Walter Benjamin for Children

JEFFREY MEHLMAN

Walter Benjamin for Children

An Essay on His Radio Years

THE UNIVERSITY OF CHICAGO PRESS

CHICAGO AND LONDON

Jeffrey Mehlman is professor of
Foreign Languages and Literature at Boston University.

The University of Chicago Press, Chicago 60637
The University of Chicago Press, Ltd., London
© 1993 by The University of Chicago
All rights reserved. Published 1993
Printed in the United States of America

02 01 00 99 98 97 96 95 94 93   1 2 3 4 5

ISBN 0–226–51865–5 (cloth)

Library of Congress Cataloging-in-Publication Data

Mehlman, Jeffrey.
  Walter Benjamin for children / Jeffrey Mehlman.
    p.   cm.
  Includes bibliographical references and index.
  1. Benjamin, Walter, 1892–1940—Criticism and interpretation.
2. Radio programs for children—Germany—Frankfurt am Main—History.
I. Title.
PT2603.E455Z734   1993
838'.91209—dc20   92-28496

For Alicia

for Natalia and Ezra

CONTENTS

1

From 1929 to 1933, in Germany, Walter Benjamin, the intractability of whose major texts has long been the stuff of literary legend, wrote—and broadcast—scripts for two radio programs for children.[1] Some thirty of those scripts, on the order of fireside chats, were abandoned in Paris by Benjamin, in 1940, only to be accidentally packed up with the archives of the *Pariser Tageszeitung,* once the Nazis themselves were obliged to flee the city.[2] An act of sabotage by the editor of the German newspaper was all that saved the archives, and Benjamin's scripts along with them, from the destruction ordered by the Gestapo authorities. Whence the curious fate of these writings for children, which languished fifteen years in Russian obscurity before being returned to Germany, where they were received, around 1960, by the Central Archives of Potsdam. It was not until 1985, however, that the scripts were finally published, in Germany, under the title *Aufklärung für Kinder,* and it is in part in order to demonstrate the odd inappropriateness of collecting them under the banner of Enlightenment that these pages, a speculative analysis of what may be at stake in Benjamin's scripts for children, were written.[3]

The piquancy of the very existence of these texts, of course, is a function of the legendary difficulty of the author's prose. Why indeed should the children of Berlin and Frankfurt warm to the thought of a writer whom the German university system all but ejected for reasons of sheer incomprehensibility? In the tragedy that Benjamin's life is generally taken to have been, the incom-

prehension of the Frankfurt jury charged with evaluating his
doctoral thesis ranks second only to the rise of Nazism as a node
of embitterment.[4] Scholem reports the admission of Hans Cor-
nelius and Fritz Schultz, who had final say on Benjamin's appli-
cation for *Habilitation,* that "they did not understand a word of
his book."[5] When the "book," *The Origin of German Tragic
Drama,* finally did appear, in 1928, Hans Heinz Schaeder, who
was well disposed toward Benjamin, nonetheless regretted, in a
letter to Hofmannsthal, that "probably only a very small number
of readers will have sufficient patience and time to assimilate this
altogether personal scholasticism, obscure to the point of incomprehensibility."[6] And this was the improbable writer who, not
long after the publication of his thesis, and, admittedly, for reasons that were largely pecuniary, signed on to delight and in-
struct (if not to woo) the children of Germany over the air. The
circumstance is, at first blush, as implausible as an anthology of
fairy tales by Hegel, a child's garden of deconstruction by Derrida. And yet it is precisely that latter case, a hybrid of the
French philosopher with Robert Louis Stevenson, which gives
an indication of some of the stakes entailed in our own reading
of these deceptively simple pieces.[7] For Benjamin, I shall attempt to demonstrate, in texts that are at times as analytically
forceful as anything in what one hesitates to call his "adult" writings, comes close to offering us just such a child's garden: one
whose blooms, transplanted, much of an entire critical generation, my own, might be construed, after the fact, as having
passed its maturity cultivating.[8]

There is, it may be countered, nonetheless a certain aptness in
our author's involvement in a children's radio program. For Benjamin, in some of his most striking texts, pretended to write in
intimate contact with a dimension of childhood. *A Berlin Childhood Around 1900* is the quasi-Proustian record of a child's mythology as it comes to invest the city of the author's earliest memories. And the Arcades Project itself, Benjamin's unfinished

CHILDHOOD

magnum opus, was conceived in substantial continuity with just such a fantasia. Thus an early draft for that work evokes the experience of the (Parisian) *flâneur:* "a childhood speaks to him, which is not the past of his own youth, in all its recency, but a childhood lived far earlier, and it matters little whether that childhood be an ancestor's or his own." [9] In both cases it is as though a dream-web, woven out of the delights and misperceptions of childhood, the stuff of what Freud called the "unconscious," had come to invest less the subject's body (as in Freud) than the complex topography of a city. Archaic feelings come to nest less in the bodily orifices whose myriad comedies and tragedies Freud claimed to chart than in the portals and entrances opening unexpectedly onto the dreamworld of the arcades: "There was a 'passage du Désir'," as one note in the Project puts it.[10] And to that extent the Arcades Project itself seems less Marxian in spirit than Freudian: what is at stake is a reactivation of (childhood) dreams, with all the aura of the "kitsch" informing them, in order to effect a decisive awakening.[11] The Project, like the *flâneur,* was to be informed by an "intoxication of anamnesis." [12]

The psychoanalytic reference is of particular relevance once we turn to the performative modality of the scripts we are about to examine. For we are dealing here with the record of a contractual mandate assumed by Benjamin: to speak nonstop for twenty minutes, on schedule, before an invisible audience, from the perspective of "childhood," on any subject of his choosing. It begins to appear as though *Aufklärung für Kinder,* as it has been called, comes as close to the transcript of a psychoanalysis of Walter Benjamin as we are likely to see. The suggestion holds even in the detail of Benjamin's own dismissiveness about his radio efforts. Consider his statement in a letter to Scholem early in 1930: "as far as whatever I do for merely economic reasons is concerned, in magazines or for the radio, I no longer write out almost anything, and simply expedite such affairs through dictation." [13] The radio scripts we shall be reading were thus in important ways lacking in "composition," bereft of that "secondary elaboration" which is the ego's prime instrument of defense.

In a digression in one of his Berlin radio broadcasts, Benjamin offers a suggestive genealogy of children's toys: "Originally toys were produced by artisans, on the side, in the course of their work, as mere miniature reproductions of the objects of daily life." [14] That affirmation opens up a possibility we will see confirmed in the course of our own analyses. For these scripts at times take on the uncanny cast of Benjaminian miniatures, theoretical "toys," then, in the sense just proffered. It happens, moreover, that toys were a subject that attracted the author's attention in his philosophical mode. In a 1928 excursus, "Spielzeug und Spielen," he argues for an understanding of toys that would remove them from the "schematic indivualism" or "subjective psychology" hitherto inhibiting efforts to come to terms with them. [15] In pressing for a treatment of the phenomenon in more "collective" terms, however, he evokes a rather nonsociological mode of the collective: "Just as the perceptual universe [*Merkwelt*] of the child is shot through with traces [*Spuren*] of the older generation and must come to terms with them, so it is in his play world. It is impossible to deduce his play from some fantasy realm, a fairyland of unadulterated childhood or art. Toys, even when not imitative of adult utensils, are a coming to terms [*Auseinandersetzung*], and doubtless less of the child with adults than of adults with him." [16] The toy is thus above all that wherein the child negotiates the imposition of an adult agenda. A precarious coming to terms that is marked by a tearing apart (*Auseinander*setzung), it is shot through with the unmastered "traces" of the other. Whence the ludicrousness of any attempt to associate the role of toys with any apprenticeship in functional skills; it would be "foolish," claims Benjamin, to trace the origin of the baby rattle to the development of the sense of hearing; rather was it, in its inception, an instrument placed in the hands of the newborn as a defense against evil spirits. [17] Now this disqualification of the functional (or instinctual) in favor of understanding in terms of the potentially traumatic negotiation of an alien (and often unconscious) agenda imposed by adults tellingly recasts a crucial (but elusive) node in Freud's own thought, wherein the (intersubjective) genesis of the "drive," as it comes to supplant and denature the "instinct," is seen to be superimposable on a modification of the "seduction theory." [18] What denatures or "perverts" the instinct, that is, is precisely the alien (and often unconscious) parental agenda as it impinges on the child. For Benjamin, toys, it would seem, would always already have been the medium of a play-analysis. It is only toward the end of the essay that Freud's name appears, in reference to the "obscure compulsion to repetition" that appears to be the motive-force behind play: repetition as the domestication of trauma, its transformation by way of habituation. [19] Beyond Benjamin's somewhat academic reference to *Beyond the Pleasure Principle,* however, what is significant is the author's insistence on repetition (*Wiederholung*) in opposition to imitation (*Nachahmung*) as the grounding virtue of play. For imitation (of parents) is the stuff of narcissism, the subjectivist psychologizing that Benjamin seems intent on keeping at bay. [20] Whereas repetition, however oriented toward mastery, retains its traumatic or catastrophic valence to the end. Such, at least, is the reading sustained by the final statement of the piece: "If, though, a modern poet maintains that there exists for each individual an image around which the entire world appears to founder [*versinkt*], for how many does that image not rise out of an old toy chest?" [21] The toy survives, but also provokes a sinking away of the world itself: it remains forever linked to the disruptive potential of the unconscious.

The "theory" of our theoretical toy-texts, then, beyond even their potential as reduced versions of Benjamin's more celebrated essays, would appear, at some level, to be psychoanalytic. Whereby we encounter anew a suggestion prompted by a consideration of the performative status of these radio scripts: *Aufklärung für Kinder,* an adult's on-schedule, nonstop, virtually unedited discourse of and for childhood, as the closest we can hope to come to the transcript of a psychoanalysis of Walter Benjamin.

Toys, however, were not the only memorabilia of childhood to have captivated Benjamin's imagination. He was an avid collector of children's books, which no doubt, as Scholem notes, helped spark his sense of the emblematical.[22] Moreover, he composed an essay on children's books of which he thought sufficiently well to select it (and only three others) for submission to Judah Magnes as part of the dossier on which he hoped to be awarded financial backing by the Hebrew University.[23] In the present context the interest of the essay, "Aussicht ins Kinderbuch" (1926), lies in its preoccupation with the very materiality of textual transformation. Words appear in costume; children are caught up in a "masquerade" of script in which meaning itself, insofar as it inhibits the scriptural whirl, functions as a form of "censorship": "Children, when thinking up stories, are stage managers, who do not allow themselves to be censored by meaning [*die sich vom 'Sinn' nicht zensieren lassen*]."[24] The point is registered in a striking evocation of rebuses. To the extent that they require interpretation, they "ring in the Ash Wednesday of the scripturo-verbal carnival."[25] Meaning per se brings the transformative feast to a close. Benjamin here approaches the Freud who, in a 1925 footnote to *The Interpretation of Dreams,* insisted that it was the dreamwork, rather than any latent meaning, which constituted the dream's "essence."[26] And it may indeed be suggested that Benjamin's essay on the transformative materiality of children's books is his own idiosyncratic take on those "primary processes" Freud grouped under the heading of "dreamwork." Shifting page orders, hidden flaps behind which lurk unexpected figures, episodes triggered or resolved through a readerly tug of a ribbon or tab: all these are among the techniques for unbinding the energies of the text whose usefulness our reading of *Aufklärung für Kinder* will attempt to establish.

Many a critic of my own generation, haunted by the unfulfillment that seems the mark of our author's career, cannot but have nursed the dream of making his own work a prolongation of what was cut short in the writing of Benjamin. This is no doubt particularly the case for those of us who have imagined—and imagined awakening from—the dream of France.[27] Benjamin himself, of course, believed toward the end that he would be bringing his thoughts (on Baudelaire, on Paris) to completion, under the auspices of the Institute for Social Research, in New York. In October 1938, we find him, in a letter to Adorno, studying the details of a map of Manhattan displayed on the bedroom wall of Brecht's son, Stefan, in their retreat in Denmark.[28] It is perhaps that letter which best illuminates the enigmatic title, *Zentralpark*, which Benjamin assigned to a collection of fragments on Baudelaire.[29] Was Central Park not to be the new Tiergarten, an arena in which—"dialectically," he thought—to dream the solution to the various literary and philosophical dilemmas facing him? For those who, like myself, spent our childhoods playing in Central Park during the very years Benjamin might have been bringing the Arcades Project to some manner of completion, criticism will always have been something of a family romance. I suggested earlier that Benjamin's radio scripts for children, properly read, were such that one might be inclined, after the fact, to imagine many a critical career as an extrapolation of formulations found in these cunningly simple texts. Walter Benjamin, that is, was not merely the absence in whose shadow, in Central Park, we played. He was a *raconteur,* an entertainer of children with words we never heard, but which, after the fact, may be read, such is my intent, as an unsuspected matrix out of which much of what is most forceful in contemporary criticism may be derived.

Benjamin in America? The pathos of that thwarted eventuality shall serve as our introduction to the text of his radio scripts. It is a twenty-minute excursus on bootleggers during the American Prohibition era, which had not yet run its course, and leads our broadcaster to tell his youthful audience a rather "pretty story" which takes place in a train station in the vicinity of New Orleans:

Young black boys move alongside a train, which has just come to a
stop, concealing beneath their clothes containers of various shape on
which may be read in large letters: iced tea [*Kalter Tee*]. After signal-
ing to a vendor, a traveler, for the price of a suit, buys himself one of
the flasks, which he adroitly conceals. Then a second one, then ten
more, then twenty, or fifty. "Ladies and gentlemen," the black boys
implore, "wait for the train to leave before drinking your tea [*trinken
Sie den Tee erst wenn der Zug fährt*]." Everyone winks complici-
tously. . . . The whistle blows, the train starts up, and all the passengers raise their containers to their lips. But disappointment soon
clouds their faces, for what they are drinking is indeed iced tea.[30]

The piquancy of the story lies no doubt in its ability to make its
assault on literal meaning coincide with the disappointing sensation of the tea trickling miserably down the alcohol-parched
throats of the hoodwinked drinkers. The flasks marked "tea" do
indeed contain what they say they do, but the congruence between name and thing, rather than confirming any natural or
proper order, is revealed to be the result of a double displacement or betrayal: alcohol for "tea," but then (in what is not a
mere reversal) tea for "alcohol". . . . Transparently literal meaning, it is suggested, is the precarious result of a particularly
opaque bit of double-dealing, and that devastating lesson is vis-
ited on the very organ of human speech: the throat. The reader
will no doubt be reminded of the closest Freudian parallel to the
Benjamin tale, an anecdote collected in *Der Witz*. Two Jews meet
in a railway carriage; questioned by the first as to where he is
going, the second replies: "To Cracow." Whereupon the first
calls him a liar: "If you say you're going to Cracow, you want me
to believe you're going to Lemberg. But I know that in fact
you're going to Cracow. So why are you lying to me?"[31] Again, a
literally true statement is shown, by way of double displacement
("Cracow" to Lemberg, then "Lemberg" to Cracow), to be *essentially* untrue. Or as the editors of the Standard Edition put it,
with admirable concision, in their index: "Truth a lie."[32]

But if we have begun our reading of the radio scripts with this
tale of bootlegging, it is less for its affinity with the Freud joke
than for its fundamental links with more familiar items in the

Benjamin corpus. The first of these that we shall consider is the most successful of his forays into the genre of the short story, "Rastelli erzählt. . . ." It is the tale of an idiosyncratic juggler, whose genius consists in his unprecedented manipulation of a single ball. "Those who had seen the master at work had the impression that he was playing with a live accomplice—alternately docile and recalcitrant, tender and mocking, obliging and faltering—rather than with a lifeless object."[33] In point of fact, the "master"'s secret, or fraud, is that his ball is, or at least contains, a living being. His accomplice is a dwarf, who is secretly hidden inside the ball, and is able to activate it through a complex system of internal springs. The tale recounts the juggler's greatest (and riskiest) performance. Before a notoriously capricious sultan, a cruel despot, he gives the performance of his life. It is only upon leaving the theater, that he is handed—late—the following sealed message from the dwarf: "Dear master, don't be angry with me. Today, you will not be able to appear before the sultan. I am ill and cannot leave my bed."[34] "Rastelli erzählt . . ." is thus a tale of a deceiver deceived in the course of his own deception. In this it resembles the bootlegging anecdote, which we shall call the "Tea-Train" or "Teezug." Whereas the "master" planned to deceive the sultan with the help of his dwarf, the white passengers on the Southern train would flout the law with the assistance of their "little black boys" [*kleine Negerlein*]. Intentionally in the "Teezug," unintentionally in "Rastelli erzählt . . . ," the accomplice fails his "master." The result in each case is the "master"'s shock that things are what they seem, his realization of just how devious a concatenation of errors and misperceptions has resulted in what may be called, in the case of "Rastelli erzählt . . . ," the miracle of "truth." The "master"'s unbelievable performance *was* as genuine as it appeared; the flask marked "Iced Tea" did indeed contain that beverage; and in each case the protagonist's sense of mastery has come decisively undone.

If "Der Teezug," as we have called it, joins up with Benjamin's fiction by way of "Rastelli erzählt . . . ," it converges with his critical writing proper by way of his celebrated essay on Kafka. That piece begins with an exemplary fable, said to herald the entirety of Kafka's achievement.[35] Chancellor Potemkin, lapsing into one of his periodic depressions, has the court of Catherine the Great in disarray. In his refusal to sign, or even consider, any offical edicts, he has paralyzed the machinery of government. An insignificant clerk, Shuvalkin, comes up with a solution. Entering Potemkin's darkened chamber, he inserts a pen in the chancellor's hand, sets a stack of edicts on his lap, and all but pushes his pen as Potemkin, in a trance, signs document after document. It is only upon emerging from the chancellor's chamber, with the sheaf of signed edicts under his arm, that Shuvalkin and the assembled councillors discover that the documents have been signed, one after the other, Shuvalkin . . . Shuvalkin . . . Shuvalkin. . . . [36] Once again, the deceiver, Shuvalkin, is revealed, after the fact, to be deceived in the course of his own deception. The signature engineered, if not quite written, by Shuvalkin reads: Shuvalkin. The flask marked, "iced tea," that is, contains no other beverage. And once again, the normality of that result is the issue of a double deception: Shuvalkin's initiative for Potemkin's, the clerk's name for the chancellor's.

"Der Teezug," then, as our two superimpositions reveal, ramifies through both Benjamin's fiction and his criticism. Indeed one might speculate that the tale, in its nodality, may find its site precisely in a region where that distinction fails to hold. But there is another Benjaminian dichotomy that the radio tale of bootlegging appears to ignore. It may be approached by way of what I take to be Benjamin's principal source for "Rastelli erzählt . . . ," Baudelaire's prose poem, "Une mort héroïque." For the Frenchman's piece similarly concerns a command performance before a despot, by a superb artist, under probable threat of death. Fancioulle, an actor, has been found guilty of conspiring against his prince. His chance for a pardon seems contingent on a command performance the prince surprisingly orders him to give. He is superb: the prince (or master) seems to be succumbing dialectically to the aesthetic power of his buffoon (or slave).

The dialectic, however, is brought to a standstill, when the prince orders a page to rush off to a far corner of the theater and deliver an ear-splitting whistle (*coup de sifflet*) during one of the buffoon's most sublime moments.[37] "Fancioulle, stunned, awakened in the middle of his dream, at first closed his eyes, then opened them again, excessively wide, then opened his mouth as if to breathe convulsively, teetered a few steps forward, a few back, then fell stone dead on the stage."[38] The dialectic has been cut short by the untimely blast of the page's whistle. But this disruption of the mastery of the master performer, in the course of (or immediately following) his most sublime achievement, a command performance given under (probable) threat of death, is the substance of Benjamin's debt to Baudelaire's "Une mort héroïque" in "Rastelli erzählt. . . ." It is an end to the dialectic (of truth, of history, of history as truth) which Benjamin captures nicely in the final words—attributed to his narrator, Rastelli, the famous juggler—of his tale: "You see, said Rastelli, after a moment of silence, that our art does not date from yesterday and that we too have our history, or at least our stories (*unsere Geschichten*]."[39] A plurality of tales invests the "truth" of history.

"Der Teezug," then, ramifies through Rastelli's tale to Baudelaire, even as it communes with Kafka by way of its affinities with the Shuvalkin anecdote. But Baudelaire and Kafka are also metonyms for the twin propensities of our "Janus-faced" thinker: the world of the Paris Arcades, centered on Baudelaire, on the one hand, and a relation to Judaism, to which his principal literary access remained Kafka, on the other. The radio tale of bootlegging, that is, however slight in appearance, in bridging what Scholem called the "severe and finally irreconcilable competition" between the author's two spheres of endeavor, has a nodality in Benjamin's work which we will do well to retain and return to in the course of our reading.[40]

What of its situation within the sum total of the scripts of *Aufklärung für Kinder?* Our best access to an answer is by way of the radio talk entitled "Die Eisenbahnkatastrophe vom Firth of Tay."[41] The piece is centrally a meditation on an early railroad disaster, the fall, on 28 December 1879, of a passenger train from a collapsed railroad bridge as it crossed the estuary (or firth) of the River Tay in Scotland. The bridge over the Firth of Tay had in fact made its way into an early draft for the Arcades Project, where it is treated as a significant moment in the history of the development of construction in iron: "Theoretical struggles were accompanied by practical struggles with matter. The history of the construction of the bridge over the Firth of Tay is a particularly striking case. Work on the bridge lasted seven years, from 1872 to 1878. And shortly before its completion, on 2 February 1877, two of the bridge's principal piers were swept away by one of those storms that burst with unimaginable violence in that region and which also provoked the catastrophe of 1879." [42] The radio script, centered on that catastrophe, situates it significantly in an identical context. Benjamin tells his audience that his aim is to locate the accident within "the history of technology [*die Geschichte der Technik*]," and particularly in that of "metal construction [*das Eisenbau*]." [43]

Iron, we read in the first Arcades "exposé," was the first "artificial" construction material to be used in the history of architecture. [44] As such, we read in the radio script, it enjoyed a certain apparent gratuitousness: "The first constructions of this type were in the order of amusements. Metal construction was tried out in winter gardens and arcades, that is in luxury edifices. . . ." [45] Benjamin then moves on to the polemic that greeted early speculation about railway travel. The medical faculty of Erlangen was resolutely opposed: "the speed would inevitably provoke cerebral lesions in passengers, and there would be a risk of fainting from the mere sight of such meteors hurtling past." [46] The dehumanizing speed of train travel was similarly denounced, we read, by an English expert: "Moving by train, he said, is no longer traveling, but simply being dispatched to a destination, like a package." [47] These are the most striking quotations chosen by Benjamin for his young audience from the archives of what he elsewhere calls the nineteenth century's "defective reception of technology." [48]

As for the "catastrophe" proper, the careening of the train into the icy waters of the Tay, Benjamin, no doubt, would have wanted to quote the testimony of a witness. Such, we shall see, is his tendency in other scripts. But eyewitnesses, we are told, did not exist; nor did anyone survive the wreck. We are given instead a fragment from Theodor Fontane's poem, "Die Brück' am Tay." Johnny at the engine defies the storm:

> Und wie's auch rast und ringt und rennt,
> Wir kriegen es unter, das Element.

(And however it rages, struggles and runs / We get the better of the element.)[49]

Johnny recalls the bitterness of his isolation, before the bridge was built, from Christmas celebrations on the other side of the river. Then, in a brief illumination, heaven seems to wreak its revenge on man's technological hubris:

> Denn wütender wurde der Winde Spiel,
> Und jetzt, als ob Feuer vom Himmel fiel'
> Erglüht es in niederschiessender Pracht
> Uberm Wasser unten. . . . Und wieder ist Nacht.

(More frenzied still the winds became / And now, as though fire fell from heaven / It glows in downward-shooting splendor / Over the water below. . . . And again it is night.)

Since there were no survivors, the circumstances under which the accident was discovered are particularly interesting. A distant flash of light (*Feuerschein*) had indeed been perceived by three fishermen, but they failed to realize that its source was the locomotive hurtling into the Tay. It was only after telegraph communication had been lost with the northern shore that a train was sent out at night to verify the condition of the wire cables attached to the bridge. Only a sudden slamming of the brakes prevented a second catastrophe: the conductor "had noticed, in the moonlight, a gaping hole [*eine klaffende Lücke*]. The central part of the bridge had disappeared."[50] It is that gap—in communication—which will allow us in turn to bridge the distance between Benjamin's *Teezug* and what one is hard put not to call his *Tayzug*. For the iced tea—the Kalter Tee—swallowed by the hoodwinked imbibers on the train outside New Orleans also effected a certain gap in communication: the double displacement that seemed to be the devastating condition of literal speech. In his first Arcades "Exposé," Benjamin, writing of the use of iron as a building material, the whole area of endeavor for which railroads served as a "precursor," quotes Siegfried Giedion: "Building plays the role of the subconscious."[51] Might it then be the case that the rift in communication we have located in both "Teezug" and "Tayzug" figures something in the order of a notion of the unconscious?

That suggestion receives support from Benjamin's coda to his radio script on the railway accident. It is an evocation of the Eiffel Tower, steel construction's own monument to itself, which was erected some ten years after the collapse of the bridge over the Tay: "At the time of its creation, the Eiffel Tower was not conceived for any use; it was a mere emblem, one of the world's wonders, as the saying goes. But then radio transmission was invented, and all of a sudden the edifice had a meaning [*Mit einem Schlage hatte der grosse Bau seinen guten Sinn*]. Today the Eiffel Tower is Paris' transmitter."[52] The broadcaster implies that meaning proper (*guter Sinn*) is very much an aftereffect. The Tay catastrophe, but also a certain gratuitousness, crucially precedes broadcasts or messages such as the one Benjamin found himself sending out in his own voice over the air waves. Perhaps we are invited to hear that catastrophe, the gaping hole in the bridge, inhering in Benjamin's words as their very condition of possibility. But no more so than the double displacement issuing in literal meaning on Benjamin's Teezug.

In superimposing "Tayzug" and "Teezug," the ice-cold Tay that swallows and the swallowing of ice-cold tea, we have effected a translation of a tale of fraud as a tale of catastrophe. And we have done so no doubt in terms corresponding to a particularly enigmatic formulation in "The Task of the Translator." "For if the sentence is the wall before the language of the original, literality [*Wörtlichkeit*] is the arcade."[53] Translation, that is,

must succeed in a realm disruptive of meaning: Teezug for Tayzug. Benjamin, remarked Hannah Arendt, regarded truth as an
exclusively acoustical phenomenon.[54]

Perhaps, in making our two tales rhyme, we may be accused
of resorting to a child's reception of these scripts (for children).
But only in the sense that the child, in Benjamin's essay on Karl
Kraus, is regarded as justified in recognizing that "by rhyme he
has reached the summit of language."[55] In "Tayzug," then, to
evoke the argument from the same essay, we have, as it were,
called the word "Teezug" "by its name."[56] What remains, however, is to determine what meaning is to be given to the apparent
translatability of these tales of fraud and catastrophe. For the
radio scripts of *Aufklärung für Kinder,* we shall see, contain a
series of tales of fraud as well as a series of recountings of catastrophes. Before essaying an interpretation of whatever relation
may inhere between the two sequences, we shall undertake to
ascertain whether the apparent translatability we have established in the case of "Teezug" and "Tayzug" can indeed be generalized.

Perhaps the most remarkable chronicle of fraud in the collection is "Briefmarkenschwindel," a script devoted to forgery and
other forms of dishonesty among philatelists.[57] In fact, however,
what gives the script its piquancy is its treatment of an interme-
diate realm, neither stamp nor forgery, but that postal supplement to the stamp which simultaneously validates and obliter-
ates it: the postmark. When philately was launched on the
market of collecting passions, a number of small states decided
to capitalize on the phenomenon by reissuing sheets of their own
rarest stamps, with the intent of selling them directly to inves-
tors. States had in effect become the forgers or self-plagiarists of
their own most prized publications. To counter this inflationary
trend, Benjamin notes, many a collector was inclined to adopt
the maxim: "this stamp is phony, because it has not been cancelled [*Diese Marke ist falsch, weil sie nicht gestempelt ist*]."[58]
And yet nothing could be more misleading than such a principle.
For a postmark can be still more easily forged than a stamp.

Indeed the special usefulness of the postmark for a forger is that it will allow him to mask whatever weak spot or imperfection might remain in his forgery. Thus a more dependable principle for the collector would reverse the earlier maxim: "this stamp is cancelled because it is phony [*diese Marke ist gestempelt, weil sie falsch ist*]." [59] Between the English couplet (stamp/postmark) and the German (*Briefmark/Stempel*) an odd chiasmus surfaces, and it is within the contours of its configuration that Benjamin's script appears to pursue its argument. The two maxims proffered in the text—the postmark as both validating supplement or completion and seal of inauthenticity—are kept in suspension throughout the text, endowing it with an unresolvable ambiguity.

The undecidable status of the postmark, the manner in which stamps are "stamped," erupts anew upon discussion of the latest bit of deviousness in the forging community. It consists of what amounts to a low-risk wholesale operation in which forgers sell their copies for a modest price on the understanding that they are not genuine but of scholarly or "scientific [*wissenschaftlich*]" value. [60] They are thus exempted from any criminal liability. Their clients, on the other hand, are then free to begin their retail trade of what they can now pass off as genuine stamps at exorbitant prices. To counter this trend it is suggested that bona fide stamps be marked with a seal of authenticity (*Echtheitsabstempelung*) underwritten by a respected trading house. [61] The objection, however, is not long in coming: "however miniscule, a commercial marking would disfigure [*entstellen*] a genuine stamp." It would be far better to affix a seal of invalidation (*Fälschungsstempel*) on counterfeit items. [62] Once again, undecidability is the feature of the postal imprint.

The postmark or cancellation is thus a third term, neither stamp nor forgery, completely unfixable on one side or the other of their divide. But in this perhaps it represents a far more subtle and devastating threat to genuine stamps than forgeries themselves. For in view of the massive cost to state postal systems incurred by the use—effectively as currency—of counterfeit stamps, a move has been afoot, Benjamin tells us, to do away with stamps altogether and replace them with postmarks (*"Sie wollen die Abschaffung der Marken und ihren Ersatz durch Stempel erreichen"*).[63] Such indeed would be the end of the stamp, the dawning of an era, moreover, in which we may look forward to a certain elaborate perfecting of the postmark itself. The script ends by envisaging a new kind of collection: that of postmarks themselves (*Stempelsammlung*). "We can already see today how postmarks are becoming progressively more varied and complex, how they integrate words and pictures into advertisements. And the adversaries of stamps have already promised, in order to win collectors to their cause, that postmarks will be as attractively illustrated with landscapes, historical tableaux, and coats of arms as stamps have been."[64]

"Briefmarkenschwindel," with its supplanting of stamps by postmarks, the primary by the secondary, is in many ways, it will be agreed, a primer of deconstruction. America *is* deconstruction, Derrida somewhere opines, and when we recall the kind of stamp-less mail in our own daily experience which most closely approximates that imagined by Benjamin in the conclusion of his script, we may perhaps add a wry corollary to Derrida's axiom: Deconstruction, on purely formal grounds, and beyond any consideration of philosophical content, is the junk mail of literary criticism.[65] But more striking still than the affinities between Benjamin's forgotten script and deconstruction per se is the extent to which Benjamin here appears to be writing, considerably in advance, the argument of one of his most celebrated essays, "The Work of Art in the Age of Mechanical Reproduction" (1938). For that text is centrally concerned with the penetration of technical forces into the very heart of aesthetic production.[66] Even as film, in its *essential* reproducibility, appears to have crucially affected the mode of being of painting, we may say that cancellations or postmarks seem, in the radio script, on the brink of supplanting postage stamps themselves. What has decayed with the advent of photography, then film, is the "aura" of the work of art, what Benjamin characterizes as its "presence in time and space, its unique existence at the place where it happens to be." [67] But stamp collecting itself seems grounded in the aura of the rarest of stamps, "the one penny British Guiana, a temporary issue, dating from 1856, of which there remains but a single specimen [*ein einziges Exemplar*]." [68] It is the aura of that uniqueness which is ultimately dissipated by the inherent undecidability of postmarks. As Benjamin puts it in "Briefmarkenschwindel": "it is all the same entirely plausible that in the century of mechanization and technology the postage stamp may not have a very long life ahead of it." [69]

The efforts to subordinate what has been liberated by technology to aesthetic ends is one of the leitmotifs of the Arcades Exposé. "Modern style" thus "represents the final escape attempt of an art besieged, in its ivory tower, by technological realities. It mobilizes all the reserves of interiority. These find expression in the linear medium, in flowers as symbols of vegetal nature, with its sterile nudity, as opposed to the surrounding world and its technical weapons." [70] In the realm of city planning, Haussmann figures an analogous effort of aesthetic containment. His "ideal" consists in "ennobling technical necessities through pseudo-ends of an artistic stamp." [71] Baudelaire succumbed to a similar tendency through his fascination with Wagner, associated with "the notion of a total work of art intent on protecting art by making it impermeable to the evolution of technology." [72] The contribution to the discussion made by "The Work of Art in the Age of Mechanical Reproduction" concerns photography. In Benjamin's words: "cult value does not give way without resistance. It retires into an ultimate retrenchment: the human countenance." [73] The aura of art, that is, is defended from the "shock" valence of reproducibility, even within an art (photography) of mechanical reproduction, only by way of "the fleeting expression of a human face." [74] It was Atget who, around 1900, according to Benjamin, fended off this last auratic resistance by taking photographs of deserted Paris streets. Of those streets, in their emptiness, we read: "It has quite justly been said of him that he photographed them like scenes of crime." [75] That crime, it would appear, at some level corresponds to the "stamp swindle" of the title of Benjamin's radio script, or rather to that essential swindle affecting stamps not from without, but from within: in the post-marks of which we can never be quite sure whether they are signs of validation or disqualification, and which seem to be sup-planting the postage stamp per se as an institution.

What "Briefmarkenschwindel" brings to the debate is a de-constructive neutralization of the Marxist turn assumed by "The Work of Art in the Age of Mechanical Reproduction." The anti-auratic "shock" of reproducible art would lie less in its quasi-Brechtian capacity to jolt (by way of "estrangement") its viewer into political action, a suggestion implicit in the move from "rit-ual" to "politics" in "The Work of Art," than in the sheer unde-cidability of the status of that instance (figured by postmark or cancellation).[76] A Baudelairean prose poem, "Assommons les pauvres," may be of use here. The imprint of the postmark, in Benjamin's "toy" or miniature text, falls with the same impact as the final words of the dandy-narrator in Baudelaire's Nietz-schean fable. After attacking a beggar who approaches him, and thus inspiring in him that modicum of dignity that comes with any form of self-defense, the dandy tells his victim-beneficiary: "Remember, if you are indeed philanthropically inclined, that one ought to apply to all your colleagues, when they ask you for alms, the theory which I have had the *pain* [*douleur*] of trying out on your back."[77] My pain on your back; what Baudelaire's "theory" traffics in here is a certain almost unimaginable degree of displacement. It is one, I have attempted to demonstrate else-where, that is a fundamental property of the moment of violence or "shock," as Benjamin called it, in Baudelaire's prose poems, but it is also the distinguishing feature of the postmark (*Stempel*) as it comes to invest and ultimately threatens to subvert the world of stamp collecting in the radio script we have been read-ing.[78]

This is not to suggest that the Benjaminian "shock," as read in the light of "Briefmarkenschwindel," is without political thrust. "Assommons les pauvres," the prose poem we have compared it to, after all, is implicitly a polemic against the institution of philanthropy. For the author of *Zentralpark,* Baudelaire's true foil on questions of philanthropy was, of course, Victor Hugo. In an important letter to Adorno of 9 December 1938, Benjamin, in fact, wrote of elaborating a contrast between the figure of the "ragpicker [*chiffonnier*] in Baudelaire and that of the beggar [*mendiant*] in Hugo." [79]

That comparison was never developed at any length. Benjamin, that is, never made it to Central Park and the completion of his Baudelaire project. For that reason, one—who was in Central Park, playing, during those years of Benjamin's absence, and in the spirit alluded to at the beginning of these pages—is tempted to cast a digressive glance at the poem Benjamin never managed to analyze for us, Hugo's "Le Mendiant." That poem, written in 1834 and included in *Les Contemplations,* is organized around the cosmic vision on which it ends. The poet welcomes a beggar into his home but is too absorbed in assessing the poetic resonances of his own gesture to listen to what the beggar is telling him: "Et je lui répondais, pensif, et sans l'entendre." He suggests that his guest remove his cloak and hang it to dry before the hearth:

> Son manteau, tout mangé de vers, et jadis bleu,
> Etalé largement sur la chaude fournaise,
> Piqué de mille trous par la lueur de braise,
> Couvrait l'âtre, et semblait un ciel noir étoilé.

(His coat all worm-eaten and formerly blue / Spread out broadly over the warm stove / Studded with a thousand holes by the light of the embers / Covered the hearth and seemed a dark starry sky.)

By the end of the poem the poet is peering at constellations in the night sky of the humble garment. Now what is most striking about the poem is less the precise meaning—Christian or cosmic-poetic—to be assigned the heaven he appears to be contemplating than the unwitting aggressiveness of the poet's unwillingness to attend to whatever the beggar may have to say. It is a hostility that takes on a particularly sinister radiance when read along with another Hugo poem concerned with another cloak: "Le Manteau impérial." [80] In that piece, from *Les Châti-ments* (1854), Hugo calls on the bees embroidered onto the imperial cloak of his nemesis Napoleon III to fly off and attack the tyrannical emperor:

> Filles de la lumière, abeilles,
> Envolez-vous de ce manteau!
> Ruez-vous sur l'homme, guerrières!

(Daughters of light, you bees / Fly off the coat! / Hurl yourselves onto the man, you warriors!)

Thus the stars imagined through the beggar's cloak furnish a model rigorously superimposable on the murderous bees summoned to take flight from the emperor's garment. Which is to say that an auratic act of charity-qua-contemplation is superimposable on an act of violent aggression. And what lends the entire configuration its pungency, at least for this alumnus of Central Park (and *Zentralpark*), is that "Le Mendiant" 's principal evocation of the starry sky ("Piqué de mille trous par la lueur de braise") is that byword of American domestic policy in the (receding) Bush era: a thousand points of light.

If "Assommons les pauvres!" for which Hugo's "Le Mendiant" is the perfect foil, is the Baudelaire prose poem best attuned to the complexities of "Briefmarkenschwindel," the one with the clearest affinities with "The Work of Art in the Age of Mechanical Reproduction" is plainly "Perte d'auréole." For Benjamin's explicit theme, the "decay of the aura," in a text intimately linked to his ongoing work on Baudelaire, is all but translated in the title of the poet's fable about the "loss of a halo." And yet the subject of the prose poem seems only marginally related to the essay of 1938. Appearing to draw its inspiration from the "Ser Brunetto, are *you* here" of Canto XV of Dante's *Inferno,* the text begins with just such an apostrophe to a respected poet unexpectedly encountered in what is apparently a dive: "What, you here, *mon cher?* You in a house of ill fame? You the imbiber of quintessences! you, the ambrosia eater! Really, this takes me by surprise." [81] The poet explains that he accidentally allowed his halo to slide from his head while being jostled in the street and hadn't the "courage" to pick it up from the mud. What a pleasure, moreover, to imagine it on the improbable head of whoever finds it: "Think of X or of Z! It will really be a scream." [82] The eminently substitutable "X" or "Z" serve to align the prose poem with the argument of "The Work of Art in the Age of Mechanical Reproduction." But its plot is strikingly evocative of another Benjamin text, which will occupy us later, but which that affinity prompts us to adduce at this juncture: the fragment of *A Berlin Childhood Around 1900* entitled "Sexual Awakening." Benjamin there evokes a street in which, years later, he would experience the "awakening of sexual desire." [83] By implication his sexuality was to be a reactivation, after the fact, of the childhood episode the fragment recounts. Slated to accompany a relative to an unfamiliar synagogue on the Jewish New Year, young Walter loses his way, and after experiencing a "burning rush of anxiety," lapses into a strangely excited indifference. "And those two waves fused their energies irresistibly in a first great experience of pleasure: the violation of the holiday became associated with the street turned procurer, allowing me to anticipate for the first time the services with which it was to supply adult desires." [84] The quasi-religious calling willfully profaned and the desire to luxuriate in one's "fall" are common to the texts of both Benjamin and Baudelaire. The will to ascribe prototypal value to the episode seems specific to the German. Later we shall have occasion to see just how pregnant a passage "Sexual Awakening" indeed is, as though, to cite another passage from *A Berlin Childhood,* it were an "echo" which the "future had left behind." [85] For the moment let it serve as an emblem of the richness of the web of texts—in and out of Benjamin— mobilized by the radio script on swindles in philately.

"Parquetry" or "inlaid work [*Intarsien*]" is the term used by Benjamin, in the course of one of his scripts, to evoke the visual equivalent of the effect he trusts his discourse will have on his listeners.[86] No doubt his own assemblage of textual fragments is beginning to exercise a comparable effect. We began by playing off a story of fraud—the "Teezug" episode of the script on boot-legging—against an excursus on catastrophe—the "Tayzug" script—and reading each as an implicit translation of the other. We next turned to a second script on a variety of fraud—swindles in the realm of stamp-collecting—and attended to the various texts by Benjamin, then Baudelaire, and even Hugo, in the play of whose transformations it appeared to be caught or implicated. But we did so with the intent of locating a script on catastrophe in *Aufklärung für Kinder* that might relate to "Briefmarkenschwindel" in a manner homologous with the relation between "Tayzug' and "Teezug." That script, to which we shall turn presently, is entitled "Untergang von Herculaneum und Pompeji." [87]

Pompei was, it appears, a constant reference for Benjamin during his work on the Paris Arcades. To cite one of the more striking references in the Project, quoted from Victor Fournel: "Were the eruption of the Butte Montmartre to bury Paris, as Vesuvius buried Pompei, after fifteen hundred years we would be able to rediscover on our signs the history of our military triumphs as well as of our literature." [88] The Paris-Pompei metaphor in Benjamin is coherent with the intention of the Project: to attend to the French nineteenth century with such devastating precision of perception that the dream that it was—and which we continue to dream—will all but shrivel up and come undone. Precision of delineation and apocalyptic ending are the two most charged features of the European imagination's fascination with (and excavation of) Pompei, and, in a different distribution, they no doubt were central to Benjamin's own excavation of the Paris of the nineteenth century.

Moreover, our earlier suggestion that Benjamin at times appears to be casting the dream-web in which Freud draped the human body over the topography of a city finds confirmation in a stunning passage from Léon Daudet's *Paris vécu,* quoted in the

Arcades Project, and in which Paris, Lyon, and Marseille all seem slated for the fate of Pompei. Looking down on Paris from atop Sacré-Coeur, Daudet observes: "One gazes from on high at this people of palaces, monuments, houses, and hovels, which seem to have been assembled with an eye to some cataclysm, or several cataclysms, be they meteorological or social in nature." [89] The city, like Marseille and Lyon, seems to be in the grip of an unspoken "menace," on the verge of collapse. "Ultimately there is a suicidal penchant in it, and in the society it shapes, that is more alive than any instinct of self-preservation. Consequently, what is shocking when one inspects Paris, Lyon, or Marseille, from atop Sacré-Coeur, Fourvières, or Notre-Dame, is that Paris, Lyon, and Marseille have endured." [90] Thus the priority of the "death instinct" and what Freud called "primary masochism" are as surely inscribed in the French cityscape for Benjamin as they are in the human psyche (and body) for Freud. That our author should use a text by Léon Daudet, editor of the anti-Semitic newspaper *Action française,* to register that point is, moreover, not the least remarkable aspect of the passage. [91]

Daudet's book was also a model ("at least in the title of his work"), as Benjamin seems almost hesitant to admit, for the autobiographical text *A Berlin Chronicle.* [92] And it is that work which affords us an entry into the radio script on the destruction of Pompei. For even as Paris is said to have initiated Benjamin, in *A Berlin Chronicle,* into the labyrinthine potential of cities, so, in the script, is Pompei, in its present state, evoked as "the largest labyrinth, the most elaborate maze [*Irrgarten*] on earth." [93] The Paris-Pompei metaphor, that is, retains its pertinence.

In this script, as in others, Benjamin quotes at length from the testimony of a survivor. In the case of Pompei, he is, of course, well served since the letters of Pliny the Younger to Tacitus remain, he suggests, "the most celebrated in the world." [94] Here is a fragment from Pliny the Younger, whose uncle was to die fleeing toward the sea, on one aspect of the disaster: "A frightening black cloud, torn by incandescent vapors issuing in sinuosities and zigzags [*grosse gezackte Feuerströme zerrissen sie zeit-*

weise] opened into long trails of fire; these resembled lightning
[*Blitzen*], but were larger." [95] Catastrophe comes with a devastating flash or illumination from above. In this, Pompei resembles
our previous disaster, over the Firth of Tay, which was perceived
by distant fisherman only as a "flash of light [*Feuerschein*]." [96] But
what of the necessarily less thematic relation to the script on
swindling in philately, the basis for our discussing the script at
this juncture? It concerns the astonishing fidelity of the "imprints" captured by the ashes from the volcano and their similar-
ity to the remarkable "imprints" or copies of stamps that forgers
have revealed themselves capable of producing. Here, for instance, is a passage from the script on Pompei:

> the ashes nested in the creases of garments, the curves of ears, be-
> tween fingers, shafts of hair, and lips. And above all they solidified
> before the corpses decomposed, so that we possess today a series of
> faithful imprints of individuals [*eine Fülle von lebenswahren Ab-
> drücken der Menschen*], some of them having fallen while running
> and fighting off death, others waiting calmly for the end. . . . [97]

Thus it is that we today possess "the perfectly sharp and life-like
image [*vollkommen scharfe, lebenswahre Abbilder*] of individuals
who lived two thousand years ago." [98] Here, now, is a passage
from "Briefmarkenschwindel," evoking the wholesale efforts of
professional stamp-forgers:

> They send brochures to small stamp-dealers, vaunting the perfect
> reproduction [*tadellose Nachahmung*] of stamps no longer available,
> their remarkable appearance as the result of an entirely new method
> of manufacture, the mathematical precision of illustrations, sur-
> charges, color, paper, filigree, and perforations—not to mention the
> cancellations [*Abstempelungen*]. . . . [99]

It is that astonishing (*bewundenswürdig*) fidelity of reproduction, culminating in an image of what English translates as "cancellation," but French, which was closer to the author, as "oblitération," which allows our two radio scripts—one of fraud, the
other of catastrophe—to communicate with each other, and to
do so much as our (or his) "Teezug" and "Tayzug" did. [100]
    The script on Pompei is framed by two allusions one is hard

put not to examine. Early in the text, we are told of the long dormancy of Vesuvius, which allowed the "slave chieftain" Spartacus to hide on its slopes along with his entire army.[101] The suggestion that Vesuvius might be an emblem of proletarian violence and the imminent doom of the bourgeoisie seems thus to be invited. On the other hand, Benjamin concludes his script by evoking the ignorance of those caught up in the catastrophe of Pompei's destruction as to what was actually causing it. The final words of the script, evoking the graffiti discovered in Pompei, read as follows: "But among the hundreds of inscriptions, there is one which we have reason to believe is the last, and which is from the hand of a Jew or a Christian versed in such matters, who wrote on a wall, upon seeing the fire threatening the city: 'Sodom and Gomorrah'. Such is the last, uncanny [unheimliche] mural inscription of Pompei." [102] Thus the theological (and biblical) reference ends up by having the last word, supplanting whatever of Marx (or Rosa Luxemburg) might be transmitted by the earlier reference to Spartacus. Perhaps . . . But in the present context our concern is not with the relation between Marxism and Judaism in Benjamin, but, more specifically, with that between fraud and catastrophe in two scripts of Aufklärung für Kinder. And it is here that the reference to Sodom and Gomorrah is of particular interest. For our discussion of "Briefmarkenschwindel" took us to its later and more celebrated transformation, "The Work of Art in the Age of Mechanical Reproduction," and from there, by way of the theme of the "decay of the aura," to Baudelaire's prose poem "Perte d'auréole." But behind the opening question of the French text, we noted a reminiscence of the question asked by Dante ("Ser Brunetto, are you here?") in Canto XV of the Inferno. Now Brunetto's sin in Dante's scheme is sodomy, as he is forced to admit, while moving with his roving—or cruising—band through the "flaming snow" to which he is consigned.[103] Thus the reference to Sodom and Gomorrah at the end of the script on Pompei, a city buried by burning "rain," is continuous with the intertextual web at whose center we have placed the script on swindling in philately.

From "Teezug" to "Tayzug," and from "Briefmarkenschwindel" to "Untergang von Herculaneum und Pompeji," the text of fraud seems translatable as the text of catastrophe. Perhaps our invocation of Dante may serve to underwrite a preliminary interpretation. Fraud and catastrophe, after all, might be rewritten as crime and punishment. At that point, the translatability of one as the other would join up with the reading of Dante by, say, Santayana, for whom punishment, in Dante, is but a symbol of the intrinsic quality of the passion it pretends to castigate. "The punishment, [Dante] then seems to say, is nothing added; it is what the passion itself pursues; it is a fulfillment, horrifying the soul that desired it." [104] Perhaps . . . But aside from the fact that our reading of the scripts is in an altogether too preliminary a stage, Santayana's take on Dante strikes me as all too Aristotelian for an apprehension of what is at stake in Benjamin. Dante is there in our intertextual web much as a daytime residue in a dream, not at all as a tutelary presence. Rather would I take as clues for our interpretation a series of elements of which some have not yet been mentioned. The Old Testament apocalypse of Sodom and Gomorrah in the Pompei script is one. Concerning the Firth of Tay, there is the quasi-messianic (or at least "angelic") mission of the locomotive as defined in the nineteenth century by Maxime du Camp or Ludwig Pau, who is quoted by Benjamin in his essay on Eduard Fuchs: "It is quite unnecessary to become an angel since the locomotive is worth more than the finest pair of wings." [105] Finally, concerning stamp-collecting, there is a reference to the collector as kabbalist: "The pursuer of postmarks must possess like a detective information on the most notorious post offices, like an archaeologist the art of reconstructing the torsos of the most foreign place-names, and like a kabbalist an inventory of dates for an entire century." [106] Thus "kabbalism," (false) messianism, and biblical apocalypse invest our twin series of fraud and catastrophe, even as they may facilitate their apparent mutual translatability. Before developing that suggestion, however, we shall do well to expand our understanding of catastrophe in *Aufklärung für Kinder* by turning to Benjamin's script on the Enlightenment's own favorite natural disaster, the Lisbon earthquake of 1 November 1755.

From Pompei to Lisbon . . . Since the ancient city itself had been the site of an earthquake only sixteen years before being destroyed (even as it was preserved) by Vesuvius, the thematic link between the Pompei script and "Erdbeben von Lissabon" is patent.[107] Yet it is precisely on the difference between volcanos and earthquakes, as we shall see, that the Lisbon script registers its most important point. It begins with Benjamin comparing himself, in his task as radio broadcaster, to a scrupulous "pharmacist" of time: "My weights are minutes, and I must weigh them with great precision, how much of this, how much of that, so that the combination be just right."[108] His script, which will combine testimony, scientific speculation, and history, in precisely calibrated doses, thus offers a temporal equivalent of the "inlaid work" referred to earlier: twenty minutes of discourse will be required, no more and no less. (One of Benjamin's more haunting short stories, "Auf die Minute," concerns the deathly silence that ensues when a radio announcer, during his broadcast, confuses the second and minute hands on the studio clock, and is left with four sinister minutes of silence to make up.)[109]

The Lisbon earthquake has entered the European imagination largely by way of the Enlightenment debate about Providence. As Voltaire wrote to Tronchin on 24 November 1755, just three weeks after the disaster: "A cruel system of physics indeed, monsieur! One would be quite embarrassed to intuit how the laws of motion bring about such frightful disasters in *the best of all possible worlds.*"[110] The earthquake, that is, was the pretext for Voltaire's invention of what was to be the leitmotif of *Candide*. The enemy for Voltaire was Pope's would-be anesthetization of pain by way an aesthetization of experience, and the political quietism that would be its corollary:

> All Nature is but Art, unknown to thee;
> All Chance, Direction, which thou canst not see;
> All Discord, Harmony not understood;
> All partial Evil, universal Good:

And, spite of Pride, in erring Reason's spite,
One truth is clear, WHATEVER IS, IS RIGHT.[111]

Now the most striking aspect of Benjamin's pedagogical treatment of the Lisbon earthquake is his lack of interest in the Enlightenment context. Kant's fascination with the earthquake, his putative invention of seismography are mentioned in passing, but when it comes time for Benjamin to dispense his principal lesson, Kant's views are deemed erroneous. For that lesson is concerned with an opposition not between providential order and apparent evil but rather between volcanos and earthquakes. "From the Greeks to Kant and on until 1870," we read, it was believed that earthquakes were caused by gases and vapors burning in the earth's core. More recent discoveries have led to an "entirely different conclusion." Earthquakes "do not issue from the center of the Earth [*aus dem tiefsten Erdinnern*], which, still today, we imagine as being liquid or, more precisely as muddy, composed of molten mud, but are the result of phenomena within the terrestrial crust [*Vorgänge der Erdrinde*]." [112] Within the surface layer [*Schichte*], unremitting instability is the rule: "masses undergo constant displacement in order to maintain an equilibrium [*in ein Gleichgewicht miteinander zu kommen*]." Incredible tensions (*ungeheure Spannungen*) are thus generated amid the surface plates, which collide and are redistributed in the form of a new equilibrium. Such is Benjamin's treatment of what is called plate tectonics. What is most striking in it is the break with an "expressive" or volcanic model, whereby the surface would register the turbulence of an inner core. On the contrary: such recourse to expressivity proves beside the point in any serious consideration of earthquakes. That expressivity should be an illusion generated by the shifting (or kaleidoscopic) interplay of surface plates is, however, transposable as a particularly potent excursus on the nature of language and interpretation. Certainly whatever exegetic turbulence may have been generated by the entirely *superficial* contact we effected between, say, "Teezug" and "Tayzug," beyond any consideration of authorial intent, finds its allegorical figuration in the

Lisbon earthquake of 1755, as analyzed by Benjamin. It is pointedly a discussion which evokes Kant and the Enlightenment only to dismiss them as having missed the structural point: a philosophy of will remains too wed to metaphors of expression to encompass Benjamin's discourse on surface tension.

The script remarks that the Lisbon quake was unique in the extent of its repercussions, which were felt throughout Europe: the area affected, we read, was an "incredible" 2.5 million square kilometers.[113] Let that observation emblematize the importance ascribed by the author to the only point he seems eager to drive home, the deconstruction of the metaphorics of ("volcanic") expression through an appeal to the inherent violence at play within the terrestrial (or linguistic) surface. That surface, moreover, is in a constant state of greater or lesser turbulence: "The Earth quakes constantly, but so slightly that we do not sense it." [114] That final observation about Lisbon, which situates our norm as no more than a local formation in a generalized field of deviations (or earthquakes), will serve as a transition to our next script, an excursus on the Mississippi floods of 1927.

"Die Mississippi-Uberschwemmung 1927" was among the last of Benjamin's scripts to be broadcast and is in many ways the most moving.[115] It begins by evoking the linearity of the great river as it appears on the map: "You will see there a slightly meandering line, which is ultimately directed rather clearly (*ziemlich eindeutig*) from north to south. . . ."[116] That appearance of *Eindeutigkeit*, however, is known by those who frequent the river to be an illusion. For the Mississippi is "in constant movement [*in ununterbrochener Bewegung*]." [117] (In this, of course, it resembles Benjamin's "earth," in the Lisbon script, which, as we have seen, "quakes constantly.") But the constant movement of the river that interests our author is not the unidirectional flow from north to south, but the shifting of its shores, back and forth, from east to west: "its banks [*Ufer*], which perpetually shift." [118] "Ten or even fifty miles from the present contour of the river, one finds innumerable lakes, lagoons, swamps, and canals, whose shape proves they are but a part of the former riverbed, which has since been displaced to the east or the west." [119] The riverbed of the Mississippi is in a state of constant self-violation: "it is never satisfied with the bed it has hollowed out for itself." [120]

Now the opposition between the univocal or *eindeutig* flow from north to south and the catastrophic *Zweideutigkeit* by which the Mississippi regularly betrays its own bed strikingly recalls a fundamental configuration in Benjamin's difficult text of 1923, "The Task of the Translator." The Mississippi, with its meanders, as it appears on the map, resembles the work of art, with its subordinate complexities, and its subservience to a meaningful end. The enigmatic suggestion of Benjamin's essay is that there exists a "mode" of translation such that "translatability must be an essential feature of certain works." [121] Moreover, such translatability will at some level affirm its contempt for the faithful rendering of meaning: the author's "theory" is one "that looks for other things in a translation than reproduction of meaning." [122] Is not the displacement eastward and westward of the river's unstable bed homologous with the "translatability" affirmed as a crucial mode of certain works of art. It would be a kind of unbound intertextuality of the sort that allows us to translate the radio script on the flooding of the Mississippi as a rewriting of the essay on translation, or "Briefmarkenschwindel" as an unwitting pre-writing of "The Work of Art in the Age of Mechanical Reproduction." Such a relation to translatability is said to be subject to "enormous danger." [123] But if, in Hölderlin's translations of Sophocles, Benjamin's limit case, "meaning plunges from abyss to abyss until it threatens to become lost in the bottomless depths of language," is not the very image of drowning an anticipation of what will await those subject to the tragic floods of 1927 in the little-known radio script? [124]

Formally, the central problem entertained by Benjamin's script is that of the maintenance of the line's linearity, its *Eindeutigkeit*, paradoxically at the expense of the line itself. For the univocity or unidirectionality of the line is dependent on the assurance or security of its destination: the great commercial city of New Orleans. Now at a time of rising waters in the Mississippi, the authorities are said to have viewed it as imperative to protect New Orleans from flooding by dynamiting the dikes protecting rural regions abutting the river. Fascism, that is, raises its head in *Aufklärung für Kinder* in the form of the United States government forcing the poor to sacrifice their lands for the sake of the "capital [*Hauptstadt*]." [125] Transposing into the linguistic medium of "The Task of the Translator," we may say that the univocal meaning of the text, its self-presence, will always be dependent on the repression of a more fundamental "translatability." Meaning will always flow to New Orleans, (the) "capital," and, in times of crisis, essential translatability (or intertextuality), the river's movement east or west, will have to be provoked and exacerbated in order the better to safeguard that illusion. The Mississippi's movement east and west, that is, is to the apparent flow southward as Benjamin's plate tectonics, in the Lisbon script, are to the "expressivity" of the volcano.

In 1927, according to the script, the mandate to destroy the dikes was such that civil war threatened. A state of siege was declared, armed forces sent in. Herbert Hoover, a cabinet secretary at the time, was attacked during a visit to the flooded territories. All in all, Benjamin presents an image of the bourgeoisie in the process of destroying its own finest achievement. For the dike system along the Mississippi "formed part of the largest public works project undertaken by the American nation." [126] Part of the accomplishment lay in the communications system coextensive with the dikes: "An electric intelligence network links up all the stations [*verbindet alle Stationen untereinander*]." [127] The observation is noteworthy because it comes close to Freud's own characterization of the ego, in the "Project for a Scientific Psychology," as "a network [*Netz*] of cathected neurones, well facilitated in relation to one another." [128] The apparent or illusory linearity of the Mississippi, then, would be that of the ego itself, the (defensive) achievement of an internal system of communication.

At this point Benjamin relates a tragic episode in Natchez during the 1927 floods. Three brothers are stranded on a roof as

their lives appear to be slipping away from them amid the raging—and rising—torrent. Benjamin quotes the testimony of the
sole brother to have survived. At one point, when what is apparently their only hope, a passing boat, ignores their cries as it
glides by, the survivor writes: "I remember that it was as though
we had gone mad [*Ich weiss nur noch, dass wir in diesem Moment
wie toll waren*]." [129] The line occurs at a juncture in the script
corresponding to that at which the reference to Hölderlin's madness crops up in the essay on translation. But the episode of the
brothers from Natchez, unlike the first half of the script, is less
striking as an echo of "The Task of the Translator" than as an
anticipation of Benjamin's later life. For the tale goes on to tell of
the despair and ultimate suicide of one of the brothers just prior
to the arrival of a fleet of rescue vehicles. He throws his pipe into
the water before plunging in himself. " 'Farewell,' he then said,
'I've had enough.' He was never seen again, and probably didn't
even make an effort to save himself. He did not want to survive
our ruin and the death of those we loved." [130] Whereupon the
rescue fleet arrives . . . too late for the lost brother. Benjamin, to
be sure, did not wait for the final catastrophe of his flight from
the Nazis to contemplate suicide. In his "diary from the seventh
of August nineteen hundred and thirty-one to the day of his
death," he even evokes the possibility of performing the deed in
the radio studio. [131] Moreover, he was capable of comparing himself, at precisely this juncture, to "a shipwrecked man who keeps
afloat by climbing to the top of a mast that is already disintegrat-
ing. But from there he has a chance to signal for his rescue." [132]
But it was not until the flight of 1940 that that last "chance,"
which had already disappeared for brother Bill from Natchez,
was to vanish for Benjamin himself. It is hard to read the docu-
mentation surrounding Benjamin's last day without being reminded of brother Bill. Lisa Fittko, who accompanied the forty-
eight-year-old cardiac patient during the nine-hour trudge, along
the "route Lister," across the Pyrenees, that September day,
evokes Benjamin's earlier failed effort to secure passage on a boat
amid the "apocalyptic atmosphere" of Marseille 1940, with its

world of "phantasy boats" and "fable captains." [133] But a similar notation occurs in the radio episode of the brothers from Natchez: "As the boat, dark and silent, passed by, we called it a coward. Was it really a boat? To this day, I don't know. But in leaving it took our last hope with it." [134] What binds the Natchez episode most intimately to the episode of Benjamin's death is the rhythm of its conclusion. No sooner do we learn that brother Bill, in his desperation, has plunged to his death in the raging torrent than the forces of salvation become manifest: "more than fifty thousand motorboats and steamships had been commandeered. . . ." [135] Just so with Benjamin's end. Fittko's narrative ends:

> ". . . he had enough morphine on him to take his life several times over.
>   Impressed and shaken by his death, the Spanish authorities let his companions continue their travel." [136]

For Grete Freund, who had been part of the group traveling with Benjamin, "the most tragic thing was that M. Benjamin could have gone through with us." [137] The reader of the radio script on the flooding of the Mississippi has no other sense of the death of brother Bill.

"Die Mississippi-Uberschwemmung 1927" thus manages to anticipate in its second half the end of Benjamin's life even as it rewrites as a tale of the Mississippi the underlying configuration of the 1923 essay "The Task of the Translator." This capacity to shift from translating the work to prefiguring the life is an indication of just how nodal and hybrid a formation within Benjamin's *oeuvre* the radio scripts of *Aufklärung für Kinder* may be. Our more restricted aim at this stage of our reading, however, has been to test what appears to be the pattern of an alignment between tales of fraud and excurses on catastrophe in the radio scripts—"Teezug" for "Tayzug" and stamp-swindles for Pompei. It is thus to the reading of a tale of fraud translatable in terms of the Mississippi flood narrative that we now shall turn.

It occurs in "Die Bootleggers," the same script from which we excerpted our tale of the "Teezug." For much of that broadcast was devoted to the ruses resorted to by those who would transgress the fourteen-mile territorial limit off American shores, within which they would be vulnerable to seizure should they be found in possession of alcohol. The "line of demarcation [*Grenzlinie*]" was known as the "rum road [*Rumstrasse*]," and it was in its vicinity that several of the most ingeniously fraudulent exploits of the bootleggers were carried off.[138] Benjamin's reading of Prohibition, then, is imaginable as the maintenance of a theoretically inviolate line: the rum road. In that respect, it is superimposable on the apparent linearity of the Mississippi, flowing toward New Orleans, in the script on the floods of 1927. In each case the line's mode of existence was as a barrier to the overflow of a threatening liquid. Such was the purpose of the levees lining the Mississippi and such the job of the Coast Guard patrol boats assigned to preventing alcohol from entering territorial waters. Yet in the case of the river, we discovered that the line, insofar as its existence was dependent on its meaningful *end*, the commercial city of New Orleans, could be maintained only at the expense *of itself*: New Orleans could be saved only by opening the levees and flooding the farms along the river. Something strikingly similar occurs at the end of the script on bootlegging. Benjamin makes reference to recent elections in the United States, in which Prohibition played an important role. Its opponents appeared to be legion, for all men of good conscience could not but be distressed by a law so widely violated that it had come to provoke widespread contempt for the very rule of law. "The only ones unconditionally for the law were the bootleggers, since they had grown rich from it." [139] Thus the maintenance of the (rum) line was championed only by those who profited from its transgression. Indeed its only effective purpose was to ensure its own trespass. But that violation of the line by itself—an interdiction existent for the sake of its own transgression—is neatly superimposable on the linearity of the Mississippi, in the previously discussed script, which could be maintained only by *its* own self-violation: the lifting of the levees in 1927. Each line may be translated as the other, but each line, in itself, has already moved beyond itself. If the limit *containing* the waters of the Mississippi, the gin of the bootleggers, might be imagined as a vessel, that vessel exists only by virtue (or for the sake) of its own breakage. Or rather: there is no distinction between the breaking and the mending of the vessel.

The Kabbalistic image of the mending of a (broken) vessel occurs at a striking juncture in "The Task of the Translator": "Fragments of a vessel which are to be glued together must match one another in the smallest details, although they need not be like one another. In the same way, a translation, instead of resembling the meaning of the original, must lovingly and in detail incorporate the original's mode of signification, thus making both the original and the translation recognizable as fragments of a greater language, just as fragments are part of a vessel." [140] "The Task of the Translator," of course, was the very essay whose translation, after the fact, we claimed to detect in the first part of "Die Mississippi-Uberschwemmung 1927." At the same time the image just cited captures nicely the montage-like aspect of "parquetry" or inlaid work which we noted in one of the radio scripts and which seems an adequate description of our technique in these pages. For we have been aligning (or translating) fragments of Benjamin's radio scripts much as one might those of a broken vessel (which, in Benjamin's words, "must match one another," although not necessarily be like each other.)[141] We have aligned three divergent tales of fraud and shown them to be translations, in Benjamin's sense, of three tales of catastrophe: the "Teezug" and the "Tayzug"; the cancellation of stamps and the obliteration of Pompei; the apparent linearity of the Mississippi and the mode of insistence of the "rum line" under Prohibition. The reference, in the last case, to a breaking or mending of vessels, moreover, recalls to us the motifs of Kabbalistic stamp-collectors, angelic locomotives, and biblical apocalypse which had already made their way into our intertextual weave. It is those images which shall help underwrite the interpretation of the twin and interpenetrating series—of fraud and catastrophe—which we shall presently essay.

But perhaps we had best pause at this juncture to confront an apparently rhetorical question of philosophical consequence: what if the "fraud" series and the "catastrophe" series, as we have envisaged them, are less metaphors than metonyms of each other? What, that is, if the relation between them is less in the order of metamorphosis than of contiguity? The question is prompted by an anomalous script in *Aufklärung für Kinder*, the only travel report in the collection, one devoted to Naples.[142] To the extent, that is, that Naples, as we shall see, is for Benjamin a kind of swindling capital, might the relation between "fraud" and "catastrophe" not ultimately be that of the very proximity joining Naples and Pompei?

The question is of consequence, since "Neapel" is in more ways than one unique among the scripts. It is, for instance, the only one explicitly to recast for a children's audience an article already written for adults. That article, moreover, which appeared in the *Frankfurter Zeitung* in 1926 was co-authored by Asja Lacis, Benjamin's Latvian lover and conduit to Brecht and to Marxism.[143] The other text jointly written by Lacis and Benjamin, moreover, was their "Programm eines proletarischen Kindertheaters" in 1928. Which would appear to inscribe the pedagogical impetus of the children's radio scripts firmly within the purview of Benjamin's Marxist (rather than Hebraist) pursuits. In Schiller-Lerg's pat formulation, Benjamin would be "presenting reality" to his youthful audience not merely as it was, but as it "was to be transformed. . . ."[144]

Perhaps then the key text on "fraud" and "catastrophe" is to be found in the jointly written "Naples" text from which the anomalous children's script was eventually drawn:

> Everything that the foreigner desires, admires, and pays for is "Pompei." "Pompei" makes the plaster imitation of the temple ruins, the

lava necklace, and the louse-ridden person of the guide irresistible. This fetish is all the more miraculous as only a small minority of those whom it sustains have ever seen it.[145]

Thus does Pompei, metonym of catastrophe, come to figure, focus, and mediate the (Neapolitan) propensity toward swindling (*Gaunerei*).[146] It is, in Benjamin's word, a "fetish," and thereby seems already to be gesturing, from antiquity, toward the world of the Paris Arcades. But reference to the Arcades also brings us back to Naples, for it was Benjamin's visit there, for a disastrous philosophy symposium on the occasion of the seventh centennial of the University of Naples, which sent him fleeing to the National Museum of Pompei.[147] Naples-Pompei, that is, at some level figures Benjamin's desire to pursue something fundamentally *other* than academic philosophy, something, we may assume, on the order of the Arcades Project.[148]

In granting interpretive centrality to the "Naples" script, though, in allowing it (and Asja Lacis, again!) to orient Benjamin's work, in this case the radio collection, toward "proletarian education," in pinning that script to its "adult" version, might we not perhaps be sacrificing the more suggestive transformations already observed at play between the work and the scripts: between the script on stamp-swindling and "The Work of Art in the Age of Mechanical Reproduction," for example, or between the script on the flooding of the Mississippi and "The Task of the Translator"? Perhaps our best guidance in answering that question is to be found in Benjamin himself, specifically in the first of the "Theses on the Philosophy of History." In that text we find the mystery of an expert chess-playing automaton dispelled by the revelation that it is actually manned by a "little hunchback" lodged within it. Benjamin concludes: "One can imagine a philosophical counterpart to this device. The puppet called 'historical materialism' is to win all the time. It can easily be a match for anyone if it enlists the services of theology, which today, as we know, is wizened and has to keep out of sight." [149] What then, to return to our radio scripts, if a certain theology were to function as the "wizened" unconscious of whatever historical materialism might indeed be the guiding philosophy of these radio scripts? The Benjamin-Lacis manifesto for a children's theater insists too much perhaps that whatever "signal" is to be liberated in the course of the theatrical improvisations it envisages, it must not be understood in terms of the psychoanalytic category of "repression." [150] Repression, like the devil, after all, has always insisted on its own nonexistence. As for the "theology" repressed or contained by Benjamin's "historical materialism," it remains for us at this juncture to return to the radio scripts at precisely the point—between fraud and catastrophe—at which we left them before engaging the anomalous excursus on Naples. [151]

In an early draft for the Arcades Project, Benjamin hazards the following theological observation concerning the city of Paris: "When two mirrors reflect each other, Satan plays his favorite trick and (like his partner in the gaze of lovers) opens a perspective onto infinity. Whether out of divine or Satanic inspiration, Paris has a passion for mirrored perspectives." [152] Our two series, then, would mirror each other, divinely or Satanically, in a mode that might be termed Parisian. One series, that of catastrophe, has its most profound resonances, within the entirety of Benjamin's corpus, with the "Theses on the Philosophy of History," in which we are told of the angel of history: "Where we perceive a chain of events, he sees one single catastrophe, which keeps piling wreckage upon wreckage and hurls it in front of his feet." [153] Benjamin's radio audience of children, some eight or nine years earlier, must have experienced an analogous sensation. For they too seemed to be (or at least hear, in Benjamin's voice) the witnesses of "one single catastrophe": the destruction of Pompei, the earthquake in Lisbon, the railroad disaster over the Firth of Tay, the flooding of the Mississippi, the murderous fire in a theatre in Canton. The unabating catastrophe alluded to in the "Theses" is part of an ongoing meditation on messianism in that fragmented text: the redemption of the past through a "messianic cessation of happening," the blasting of what is called a "now-time [*Jetztzeit*]" out of the continuum of history.[154] For that reason, we would similarly inscribe the catastrophe series in the radio scripts under the sign of apocalyptic messianism. What then of the other series, which we have characterized as concerned with fraud? We should first note that it includes numerous more members than the two—bootlegging and stamp-swindling—we have already analyzed. There is, for instance, a script dealing with "robber bands in old Germany"; another that meditates the status of Caspar Hauser as an impostor; a third about the magical activities of the original pre-Goethean Dr. Faustus; a fourth about the infamous Cagliostro. Fraud itself is not particularly thematized in Benjamin's work. The essay on "The Storyteller" makes reference to "the traditional sympathy which storytellers have for rascals and crooks," and it may be argued that Benjamin, in his radio scripts, was no more than giving vent to that propensity.[155] But our interest here is less in the theme of fraud than in the apparent convertibility of tales of fraud into excurses on catastrophe.

We have seen, however, that the scripts on catastrophe, which jointly seem to form what the "Theses on the Philosophy of History" call "one single catastrophe," are by implication part and parcel of what would emerge as Benjamin's thought on messianism. At this point our entire configuration takes on the clarity of a puzzle on the brink of solution. For once one has eluded the temptation to read "fraud" and "catastrophe" as crime and punishment, what remains is the mutual permeability of "fraud" and a preoccupation with catastrophe we may transcribe as "messianism." But that conjunction of terms—fraud and messianism—leads directly to what was no doubt Gershom Scholem's principal (and quite idiosyncratic) preoccupation during these years, the legacy of Sabbatai Zevi, the notorious seventeenth-century "false messiah."[156]

It was a subject on which Scholem conversed with great excitement and at length during his visit to Paris in 1927. "Benjamin was the first person I told about a very surprising discovery I had made: Sabbatian theology—that is, a messianic antinomianism that had developed within Judaism in strictly Jewish concepts."[157] He goes on to describe what was for him an "unforgettable" evening at the Café Dôme in Montparnasse. Benjamin was accompanied by Franz Hessel, and Scholem spoke to them both about a leading Sabbatian theologian: "In Abraham Miguel Cardozo's writings in defense of the Sabbatian heresy, which I talked about on the basis of my Oxford studies, smoldered a flame that leaped from me to my first audience."[158] The general context of the discussion was an "entirely new turn" given by Scholem to the question of "what Judaism was all about," and Benjamin was plainly in the grip of Scholem's obsession.[159] In 1931, moreover, four years later, we find Benjamin securing a copy of Josef Kastein's book on Sabbatai Zevi for Scholem.

Having generated within Benjamin's radio scripts for children the surprising configuration of a "false" (or fraudulent) "messianism" (or preoccupation with history as catastrophe), and having located the particularly febrile circumstances under which a theory of Sabbatianism, the legacy of Judaism's "false messiah," was communicated to Benjamin by Scholem in Paris, we shall presently examine the "entirely new turn" given to the understanding of that subject by Scholem. To that end, there can be no better starting point than the lecture entitled "Sabbatianism and Mystical Heresy" in the volume Scholem dedicated posthumously to Benjamin, *Major Trends in Jewish Mysticism*.[160] In Scholem's telling, Sabbatai Zevi was a seventeenth-century "manic-depressive," given to the performance of impious acts, who was convinced by Nathan of Gaza, the young illuminate whom he came to consult for relief from his depression, that he, Sabbatai, was indeed the Messiah. Thereafter, the two toured the world of a Jewry recently devastated by the massive Chmielnitzki persecution of 1648, and Sabbatai was acclaimed by many as the savior of his people. An entire Kabbalist theology was developed by Nathan, the movement's prophet, to accommodate Sabbatai Zevi's "psychosis" to his new world historical role. Matters turned more complex, however, when the Turkish sultan, impatient with the new and subversive fervor, demanded Sabbatai Zevi's submission—in the form of conversion to Islam—under pain of death. Sabbatai Zevi, who was apparently in no way a remarkable individual, submitted in short order, thus leaving the masses who had rallied to his call with the excruciating dilemma of how to absorb the paradox of an apostate messiah.

It was at this juncture that the antinomian theology referred to by Scholem emerged in full bloom. For it consisted in accommodating the scandal of an apostate messiah, a circumstance more unsettling, after all, than even a crucified messiah, by positing that at this stage of the redemptive process it was the task of the messiah to descend into evil in order to defeat it from within. Sabbatian "radicals," in fact, pretended that theirs was the obligation to follow the example of their apostate king and stage their own divinely inspired transgressions of biblical law. It was in the logic of that proposition that apostasy itself become a Jewish imperative, and by the eighteenth century a Sabbatian leader in Poland, Jacob Frank, "the most hideous and uncanny figure in the whole history of Jewish messianism," was leading his followers in mass conversions to Catholicism.[161] Sabbatianism, that is, had become a kind of voluntary Marranoism, in which one could pretend to be all the more Jewish in that one in no way appeared to be (or act) so. Now the most surprising turn in Scholem's argument lies in his situating the Jewish Enlightenment or Haskalah not as a flight from Jewish mysticism or religion but rather as a reality enabled above all by the Sabbatian tradition of mystical transgression once the antinomian theology underlying it had faded from popular consciousness.

It is here, in the construing of Sabbatianism as the historically repressed past of rationalism, that Scholem's thought converges with Benjamin's. For even as Scholem would win back, from the meliorist ethos of rationalism, the cataclysmic or "volcanic" history in which it was grounded, so Benjamin, in the Arcades Project as well as in the "Theses on the Philosophy of History," stages an unrelenting polemic against the Enlightenment shibboleth of "progress." [162] In the Arcades Project, we read that one of the aims of the work is "the demonstration of a historical materialism that has annihilated within itself the idea of progress." [163] The numerous calls to the imperative of "blasting" or "dynamiting" one's way out of the empty homogeneity of a temporal continuum all bespeak the violence of what the (social democratic) fetishization of progress is desperate to *contain*. "Progress" is given the lie by the redemptive possibilities opened up by "a Messianic cessation of happening." [164] The unmentioned source of Benjamin's left-wing polemic against the Enlightenment notion of progress is in all probability the anarchist author of *Les Illusions du progrès*, Georges Sorel. [165] (The fact is of particular interest in view of Scholem's suggestion that "in the eighteenth century, to be called a Sabbatian was to all intents and purposes equivalent, so far as the effect on ordinary public opinion was concerned, to be termed an anarchist or nihilist in the second half of the nineteenth.") [166] By the time Benjamin was working on the Arcades Project, the tutelary thinker for the dismantling of the notion of progress had become Auguste Blanqui.

Blanqui, in prison at the end of a life of revolutionary agitation, delivered himself of what Benjamin calls a "cosmic phantasmagoria," the "last" of the nineteenth century, and which contained a devastating critique of all the others. [167] Blanqui's principal thought is that, given the infinity of time and space in the universe and the eminently finite number of elements that can be combined, it is a certainty that all the possibilities in the world are perpetually being played out in an infinite number of times and places in the cosmos. Blanqui's text, notes Benjamin, "presents the idea of eternal return ten years before *Zarathustra*, in a manner scarcely less moving and with an extreme power of hallucination." [168]

The conferring of eternal status on all that exists has as its principal casualty the notion of progress. Here is Blanqui as Benjamin quotes him in the conclusion of his second Arcades Exposé: "there is no progress. . . . What we call progress is bolted shut onto every earth and vanishes along with it. Always and everywhere in the terrestrial sphere, the same drama, the same backdrop, on the same narrow stage: a noisy humanity, infatuated with its own grandeur, believing itself to be the universe and living in its prison as though it were an immensity, only to succumb in short order along with the globe which bore—with deepest contempt—the burden of its haughtiness. The same monotony, the same changelessness on foreign stars. The universe repeats itself endlessly and swaggers in place. Eternity imperturbably offers the same performances throughout infinity." [169] Thus the notion or reality of progress is in fact a local illusion within a cosmic process of repetition that may properly be characterized as catastrophic. Blanqui's catastrophism is a function of his drawing on a modification of the notion of entropy. For all stars are perpetually on the wane; most have no doubt already died and are "floating tombs." [170] The universe, that is, is a vast *Trauerspiel*. The only way for a dead world to regain its energy and reenter the eternal return is through a cataclysmic collision with another extinguished world: "How many billions of those gray corpses crawl in like manner through the blackness of space, waiting for their hour of destruction, which will at the same time be their hour of resurrection?" [171] Further on, speaking of extinguished stars, Blanqui continues: "How might they re-ignite if not through movement transformed into heat in gigantic proportions, that is through a collision [*entrechoc*] which volatilizes them while calling them to a new existence?" [172] Thus Blanqui, in a text whose catalytic effect on Benjamin was such that the entire conclusion to the final Arcades Exposé was devoted to it. Were we to summarize the passages quoted in this paragraph, Blanqui's thought might be formulated as follows: progress as the local illusion of a universe dominated by a primordial repetition whose two principle engines are catastrophe (or cataclysm) and "resurrection." But that formulation brings us directly back to Scholem on Sabbatianism: the Haskalah (or Jewish Enlightenment) is a desperate effort to blot out an awareness of its origins in a discourse of apocalypse and resurrection, Sabbatianism. It is fitting, then, that in his most overtly

messianic texts, the "Theses," Benjamin should write of the Social Democrats: "Within three decades they managed virtually
to erase the name of Blanqui, though it had been the rallying
sound that had reverberated through the preceding century." [173]

A second link between the Sabbatian heritage (as elaborated
by Scholem) and Benjamin's thought pertains to the specifically
antinomian posture of Sabbatianism. Prior to the ascendancy of
Sabbatai Zevi, Scholem tells us, the predominant school of Kabbalah—from Safed—was a meditation on (Jewish) redemption,
liberation from the yoke of servitude, which was construed as
coterminous with a "radical change in the structure of the universe." [174] "The historical redemption is, as it were, a natural by-
product of its cosmic counterpart, and the Kabbalists never conceived the idea that a conflict might arise between the symbol
and the reality which it was supposed to express." [175] Now the
upshot of the "voluntary Marranoism" that Sabbatianism was to
become was to effect a decisive rift between symbol and symbol-
ized. The imperative, it will be recalled, was to fulfill the com-
mandments of the Torah by means of transgressing them (since
at this stage of the redemptive process evil would have to be
defeated from *within*). Under the new dispensation, one was a
good Jew precisely to the extent that one did not appear to be
one.[176] The result was what Scholem calls a "yawning chasm"
between the two spheres in the drama of Redemption: "Inner
and outer experience, inner and outer aspects of *Geulah*, of Redemption and Salvation, were suddenly and dramatically torn
apart." [177] Sabbatianism, in brief, displaced and vitiated what
Kabbalism had long taken to be the fundamentally *symbolic*
structure of reality. Enter Benjamin, who at this time may have
been in advance of Scholem's reflections. For the disjunction introduced through "allegory" into the structure of the "symbol"
is perhaps the central intuition of the thesis on *The Origin of
German Tragic Drama*. "Where man is drawn towards the symbol, allegory emerges from the depths of being to intercept the
intention, and to triumph over it." [178] Where Scholem had declared his discovery to be the existence of a full-blown antinom-

ianism in Judaism, Benjamin, in his thesis, was meditating the "antinomies of the allegorical." [179] For the scholar of Sabbatianism, the " 'believer' must not appear to be as he really is." [180] For the critic of *Trauerspiel*, "any person, any object, any relationship can mean absolutely anything else." [181] Ultimately, it was the totalizing aspiration of Lurianic Kabbalah which fell prey to the antinomies of the Sabbatians. Redemption would no longer be the "steady and unhindered progress" of divinity reinvesting the world, a mending of the primordial catastrophe of the "breaking of the vessels," but the "dangerous paradox" of an apostasy all but "incomprehensible to others." [182] Just so allegory's effect on the "image of organic totality" mediated by the "symbol." With allegorical script, writes Benjamin, "the false appearance of totality is extinguished. For the *eidos* disappears, the simile ceases to exist, and the cosmos it contained shrivels up." [183] In Scholem's Sabbatianism, then, as in Benjamin's *Trauerspiel*, the redemptive claims of a symbolic whole ("Lurianic Tikkun" or aesthetic "symbol") are crucially disarticulated by an antinomian instance (fulfillment through transgression or "allegory" itself).

A third point of contact between Sabbatianism and Benjamin's critical and philosophical work may be situated in terms of the second of the "Theses of the Philosophy of History": "The past carries with it a temporal index by which it is referred to redemption. There is a secret agreement between past generations and the present one. Our coming was expected on earth. Like every generation that preceded us, we have been endowed with a *weak* Messianic power, a power to which the past has a claim." [184] Now one of the more remarkable aspects of Scholem's delineation of the "false Messiah," as he came to be known, is what he calls "the weakness of Sabbatai Zevi's personality as compared with that of Jesus." [185] The Jewish conception of the Messiah, we are told, is "surprisingly colorless," indeed virtually "anonymous," but nowhere is that "weakness" so pronounced as in the case of Sabbatai Zevi, a man who left behind no memorable statements or "words of the master." In brief, "weak messianism" in the apocalyptic leftism of Benjamin seems to find its

counterpart in the evocation by Scholem of the "weakness" of
the Messiah figure convulsing world Jewry during the seventeenth century.

We draw our Sabbatian interlude to a temporary close by sum-
marizing where it has brought us and how we arrived there. Our
reading of the radio scripts for children of *Aufklärung für Kinder*
led us to perceive two distinct series: one concerned with tales
of fraud, the other with historical catastrophes. To our surprise,
those two series, in the three cases examined from each, revealed
the translatability of a tale of fraud into an excursus on catastrophe: Teezug into Tayzug; the role of cancellations in stamp-
swindling into the obliteration (and preservation) of Pompei; the
configuration of the "rum line" during Prohibition in the United
States into that of the Mississippi in the year of its most devastating floods. (At least two of the scripts read, moreover—"Briefmarkenschwindel" and "Die Mississippi-Uberschwemmung
1927"—were readable as significant transformations of key philosophical or critical texts by Benjamin, thus establishing the potential payoff in our reading of the scripts.) With the apparent
translatability of the fraud series as the catastrophe series, and
the thematic rootedness of catastrophe in the author's later
thought on messianism, we then proceeded to speculate on the
phantom presence of the motif of a "false messianism" in *Aufklärung für Kinder*. We were encouraged to do so, moreover, by
the fact that Sabbatianism, the antinomian legacy of Judaism's
"false messiah," Sabbatai Zevi, had become a leading preoccupation of Gershom Scholem, one that he first communicated, in
the dramatic circumstances he has evoked, to Benjamin in 1927.
Our speculation was immediately rewarded by the perception of
significant parallels between Scholem's reading of Sabbatianism
and its role in the origins of the Jewish Enlightenment, on the
one hand, and, on the other, such centrally important nodes of
Benjamin's thought as the grounding of the notion of progress in
a theory of catastrophe; the "interception" of symbol by alle-

gory; the role of "*weak* messianism" in the "Theses on the Philosophy of History."

We return to the texts of *Aufklärung für Kinder* by way of an episode reminiscent—or emblematic—of our starting point, the "Teezug" sequence in the script on bootlegging. It is taken from a script on the pre-Goethean tradition of Dr. Faustus and constitutes what Benjamin calls one of the most "extravagant [*wildesten*]" tales of magic that he knows.[186]

> One day that Faust had been invited out by a few merry chaps, they asked him to perform in their presence a magical beheading to be followed by a recapitation [*Wiederansetzen des Kopfes*]. A valet prepared for the experiment and Faust cut his head off. When he attempted to reconnect it, there was a problem, and Faust concluded that one of the guests had cast a spell on him. After admonishing his audience to no effect, since the culprit did not break his spell, Faust caused a lily to sprout from his table, whereupon he cut the flower off with a single stroke of his knife. Immediately, the head of the guest who had cast a spell on Faust became separated from his body. Faust reconnected the valet's head and proceeded on his way.[187]

It is the ability to place that much distance (and time) between head and body which recalls the situation of the hoodwinked deceivers in the script on bootlegging. The label sits on the flask of iced tea (in the "Teezug" sequence) much as the head sits (back) on the neck of the valet's body in the episode just cited. Between label and labeled, head and neck, is introduced an identical sense of the sheer arbitrariness (if not duplicity) of what had previously been taken for granted as normality itself. Thus does the Faust episode hark back to the "Teezug" and, beyond it, to the astonishment of the master juggler in "Rastelli erzählt . . ." that his "unbelievable" performance before the sultan had indeed been unbelievable.

After "Briefmarkenschwindel" and "Die Bootleggers," that is, "Dr. Faust" would thus be enterable into the series we have associated with "fraud." Lest there be any doubt, we might invoke Faust's last (and foiled) exploit in the puppet theater. Benjamin himself refers to it as a "lamentable con job [*eine ganz jämmerliche Schwindel*].[188] Hounding Faust for cash that is owed him, at a time just before the devil plans to drag Faust down to hell, an ingenuous (and Leporello-like) Harlequin is told by his debtor that, although he is without funds, he is willing, for reasons of honor, to exchange costumes with him. Since the creditor's garb is far more costly than the debtor's, surely this is an offer Harlequin will not be able to refuse. Faust's hope, that is, is to deceive the devil into mistakenly going after Harlequin, dressed up in Faust's own clothes. He fails in this, but reveals himself in the process to be a worthy member of our "fraud" series.

The first Faust tale, in its nodality, also connects with another concern in the radio scripts, the relation between science and occultism. No sooner is the beheading/reheading episode told than we are informed that "this kind of exploit had a scholarly name at the time. It was called *Magia innaturalis*, or denatured magic, to distinguish it from *Magia naturalis*, natural magic, which corresponds to our physics, chemistry, and technology."[189] Science, that is, would be a local formation, within a general economy of what all agreed was magic. The point is repeated at greater length in a radio script about witch trials ("Hexenprozesse").[190] Benjamin reports that the obsession with exterminating witches dates from the fourteenth century, a period of great scientific achievement (*die Zeit eines grossen Aufschwungs der Wissenschaften*).[191] How then to reconcile the explosion of violent superstition with the growth of scientific knowledge? "As follows: in the Middle Ages, speculative or descriptive sciences, which we call theoretical, were not distinguished from applied sciences, such as our technology. Now applied science and magic were more or less the same. So long as one did not labor in the service of evil, such magic was authorized, and to distinguish it from black magic, it was simply called white: white magic. Thus everything that was discovered about nature ended up directly or indirectly serving magical belief—in stars, in the art of producing gold, etc. And the interest in white magic rebounded into one in black magic." [192] Thus the white magic of the script on witch trials corresponds to the "natural magic" of the development on Dr. Faustus, even as "black magic" and "unnatural magic" are similarly superimposable. In both cases what modernity regards as the opposite of magic, science, is traced back to a broader economy of practices and discourses—termed magic—in which that opposition does not hold.

But Benjamin takes things a step further in the script on trials for witchcraft. He characterizes "science" in terms of the cruelty of its preoccupation with repressing "black magic," a concern which represses any awareness of its own rootedness in the broader formation termed "magic." Science would appear to be above all the science of (rooting out) black magic. Whence the fidelity of philosophers to the very "reality" they pretended to be eradicating. Whence, as well, the observation, quoted by Benjamin, of one expert in 1660: "To deny the existence [*Dasein*] of witches is to deny the existence of spirits, for witches are spirits. But to deny the existence of spirits is to deny God, since God is a spirit. Thus to deny witches is to deny God." [193] Much of the script is concerned with the cruel "obstinacy of the experts [*die Starrköpfigkeit der Gelehrten*]" in defending their bailiwick even as they pretended to be intent on doing away with it. And, to be sure, of those experts, "the worst were the jurists [*Rechtsgelehrten*]." [194] It would appear, then, that if this script can be entered into our series placed under the rubric of "fraud," it would be by virtue not of the marginalized "witches" but of the "scientists" and "experts" capable of producing the bogus juridical "wisdom" that underwrote the prosecution and execution of witches.

Beyond the humanitarian question, epistemologically, the fraud of the "white magicians" ("Hexenprozesse") or "natural magicians" ("Dr. Faust") would lie in their denial or repression of their own insertion into the discursive and practical field of "magic." Their "enlightenment," that is, is shot through with archaic if not mystical beliefs. We recognize here, transposed to a different century, the configuration of Scholem's genealogy of Enlightenment in an exacerbated mysticism, the legacy of the Sabbatians. Whence the importance for us of the script following "Hexenprozesse," and which is devoted to "robber bands in old Germany [*Räuberbanden im alten Deutschland*]." [195] For it introduces into the matrix a Jewish or Hebrew component. From a political perspective, the robber bands evoked by Benjamin are, like the witches persecuted in the previous script, a marginalized social group subject to the intolerance of a powerful state apparatus. (Indeed we are told that certain "brigands must have believed themselves to be warlocks [*Hexenmeister*] or to have concluded a pact with the devil.")[196] Yet epistemologically they may be superimposed on the witches' enemies, those pseudo-savants whose field of expertise was precisely the ravages of witchcraft. For they too are consummate practitioners of fraud. Indeed the script eventually modulates from "brigands" to the confidence tricks rampant among the denizens of what Victor Hugo, in *Notre-Dame de Paris*, made famous under the name of "Cour des miracles": for it was there that thieving beggars, pretending to be blind or lame, "miraculously" regained use of their eyes and limbs. The "brigands," in brief, like the "experts" on witchcraft in the earlier script, are members of our "fraud" series. Now one of the recurrent motifs of the script on robber bands is an affinity with Judaism. In Benjamin's words: "I would be obliged, at least for today, to pass over one of their most beautiful and important secrets [*eines der schönsten und wichtigsten Räubergeheimnisse*], their argot, and their script, known as *Rotwelsch*. The language is already quite informative as to their origin. For alongside German, it contains a good deal of Hebrew [*Es ist in diesem Rotwelsch neben dem Deutschen vor allen Dingen sehr viel Hebräisches*]. Which indicates that robbers have always been in contact with Jews. Certain Jews even became chiefs of rather formidable bands in the sixteenth and seventeenth centuries." [197] Later in the script Benjamin quotes from Luther's preface to a German-language *Liber vagatorum*, a curious volume, first published in 1509, which pretended to describe (and thus help vitiate) the deceptive world of thieves from within. Luther writes: "I deem it useful that such a book has not only been printed, but widely distributed, for it emerges clearly from it in what manner the devil governs the world, and that men are incorrigible. The book's argot [*die rotwelsche Sprache*] comes from the Jews, for it is full of Hebraic words. Those who know Hebrew will perceive as much." [198] Further on, "Kabbalistic signs" are said to have been found in the archives of the oldest robber bands.

In assembling the various elements examined from these last three scripts concerned with fraud, we thus find a rational (or pseudo-rational) discourse ("white" or "natural" magic) intent on repressing its own insertion and origins in the world of the mythic or archaic, and in significant ways derivative from practices of the Jews (and even Kabbalah). The configuration—or phantasm—is superimposable on Scholem's reading of Enlightenment as the afterbirth of a mystical antinomianism intent on forgetting its own origins. We thus again encounter the spectral presence of the "false messiah" within the *Aufklärung* or Enlightenment the editor of the radio scripts was perhaps too quick to identify as what it was the author was intent on broadcasting to children.

The point may be sustained by a consideration of what is in important ways, in this reading, the hidden center of the volume, an excursus on a genuinely false "redeemer," Cagliostro. [199] From the beginning of his script, Benjamin informs his audience that the fascination of the individual lies in the fraudulent religious eminence he achieved: "I shall speak to you today about a great confidence man [*von einem grossen Schwindler*]. Great not only because he swindled insolently and sordidly, but because he did so to perfection. His fraudulent deeds made him famous throughout all Europe; tens of thousands revered him almost as a saint, and from 1760 to 1780 his portrait—in engravings, paintings, or sculptures—was to be found everywhere." [200] Ultimately, the enigma for Benjamin is that the mystical devotion Cagliostro inspired should have occurred in the midst of a century of Enlightenment, "an age in which men were, as you know, quite distrustful of irrational traditions, confiding only, they maintained, in their own freedom of thought."[201] Cagliostro thus figures an incongruous or untimely outburst of mystical fervor in an atmosphere committed to critical thinking. From the perspective of (Scholem's reading of) Sabbatianism, it is as though Cagliostro represented a return of the repressed.

But Cagliostro, it will be countered, was in no way a Jew, and certainly Benjamin does not suggest he was. A profound relation to Judaism was nonetheless a crucial ingredient of the tradition surrounding the "scoundrel-genius" throughout the nineteenth century. That last characterization of Cagliostro was by Thomas Carlyle in his *Miscellaneous Essays,* and we shall be drawing on his Cagliostro essay, as well as on Gérard de Nerval's in what follows.[202] For Nerval, for example, Cagliostro and the count of Saint-Germain, though Christian, were "the most celebrated Kabbalists of the end of the eighteenth century."[203] The Carlyle essay on the figure is studded with references to Cagliostro's reputed Judaism. His speech, wrote Carlyle, was a "Tower-of-Babel jargon, which made many think him a kind of Jew."[204] And further on: "*Is* he the Wandering Jew, then? Heaven knows!"[205] The Hebraic reference, however, went beyond mere rumor. In the ritual of what became virtually his own Freemason sect, instructions were issued concerning "how you have to choose a solitary mountain, and call it Sinai; and build a Pavilion on it to be named Sion, with twelve sides."[206]

Benjamin himself refers in passing to Cagliostro's "phantasmagoria [*Phantasievorstellung*]" concerning the existence of a Seventh Book of Moses.[207] Beyond that observation, however, Carlyle, drawing on a biography of the "Quack of Quacks" prepared by a member of the Inquisition, adds a remarkable wrinkle to Cagliostro's relation to the Hebrew prophet:[208] "Here, however, a fact rather suddenly transpires, which, as the Inquisition-Biographer well urges, must serve to undeceive all believers in Cagliostro; at least, call a blush to their cheeks. It seems: 'The Grand Cophta, the restorer, the propagator of

Egyptian Masonry, Count Cagliostro himself, testifies, in most part of his System, the profoundest respect for the Patriarch Moses: *and yet* this same Cagliostro affirmed before his judges that he had always felt the insurmountablest antipathy to Moses. . . .' How reconcile these two inconsistencies? Ay, how?"[209] Cagliostro's Old Testament faith is thus internally at odds with itself, a Mosaic anti-Mosaic antinomianism. But to have acknowledged as much is to have brought the enigmatic figure of "Count Proteus-Incognito," as Carlyle calls him, in extraordinary proximity to Scholem's reading of Sabbatianism.[210] For the Sabbatian precept that "the subversion of the Torah can become its true fulfillment" is informed by an identically Mosaic anti-Mosaic ambivalence.[211]

The parallel continues still further. Toward the end of his radio script, Benjamin recounts the bizarre event triggering Cagliostro's downfall: "He had somewhere written that in Medina, from which he was alleged to come, the inhabitants had rid themselves of lions, tigers, and leopards by stuffing their pigs with arsenic and then letting them loose in the forest, where they were devoured by wild beasts, thus provoking their death. Morand, the publisher of the *Europäischer Kurier*, printed the item in his newspaper. Cagliostro was quite vexed and issued him a bizarre challenge. On September 3, 1786, he published an invitation, in which he called on Morand to share with him, on November 9, a suckling pig stuffed with arsenic, and bet five thousand florins that Morand—and not he himself—would die as a result."[212] Morand rejects the invitation and ends up orchestrating a campaign of rumors against Cagliostro which eventually leads to his imprisonment by the Inquisition in Rome. Before commenting on this bizarre final episode, in which the self-styled count challenges his adversary to dine on arsenic-laced pork with himself, we would complete it by recalling a sequence that Carlyle refers to as the effective beginning of his hero's life of fraud. Cagliostro, whom Carlyle refers to in the Sicilian diminutive Beppo, undertakes to fleece "a certain ninny of a Goldsmith named Marano."[213] Marano is lured to a mine where he is attacked by stooges hired for that purpose by "Beppo." "Six Devils pounce upon the poor sheep Goldsmith and beat him almost to *mutton*."[214] Goldsmith, however, having come to the assignation armed with a stiletto, is able to repulse his assailants; the theft comes to nought; and Cagliostro is forced to flee . . . into a life of fraudulence. Now Carlyle's insistence on sheep and (italicized) mutton appears almost willfully to distract the reader from recalling that "mar(r)ano" means pig in Spanish. Thus Cagliostro's career in "scoundrelism" was framed by two episodes centered on "pigs." Let us consider the earlier of the two first. "Marrano," of course, also means *converso*, a converted Jew who secretly continued to keep his abandoned faith. It was for that reason, we saw, that Scholem was able to refer to Sabbatianism as a kind of "voluntary Marranism."[215] To the extent that the idea of an "apostate Messiah" could be presented to self-doubting or self-loathing Marranos as "the religious glorification of the very act which continued to torment their own conscience," the Marranos themselves were subject to a spiritual exploitation (or "fleecing") every bit as devastating as what Cagliostro had in mind for his "Marano."[216] Consider now the second (and final) pig-related episode: bizarrely, the count challenges his adversary to share a poisoned pork with him. We can, of course, not be sure whether Cagliostro was bluffing (and would have backed down) or calling his enemy's bluff. The episode, as recounted by Benjamin, seems almost drawn from a dream. But of what? It is at this juncture that one is inclined to recall that for an observant Jew pork is *always* poisoned, a violation of biblical dietary law. Thus the public and almost ceremonial consumption of pork, a food which is *essentially* (because spiritually) poisoned takes on the appearance of a transgressive ritual. It is one that might well be informed by the Sabbatian maxim of the Law fulfilled through its own transgression.[217] Thus our two pig-related episodes, the beginning and end of Cagliostro's career, take on an odd coherence within the interpretation of Sabbatianism proposed by Scholem: the spiritual fleecing of what might anachronistically be called a Marrano pride movement by way of public displays of ritual transgression (and eventually apostasy).

For Nerval, Cagliostro the Kabbalist merits an important role in any understanding of the advent of the French Revolution. Indeed the first section of his essay on the "Count" in *Les Illuminés* is entitled "Du mysticisme révolutionnaire," and throughout his treatment of "the celebrated Kabbalist," whom he (unlike Carlyle) in no way sees as a "quack," reference is made to the debt of the revolutionaries to "the primitive doctrine of the Hebrews." [218] The point is significant since Scholem, on several occasions, brings his history of Sabbatianism into contact with the events of the French Revolution. Jacob Frank, an eighteenth-century leader of radical Sabbatianism in Poland and "one of the most frightening phenomena in the whole of Jewish history," led his entire flock into mass-conversion to Catholicism. [219] Scholem notes that Frank's nephews were active in high revolutionary circles in Paris and Strasbourg. "Seemingly, the Revolution had come to corroborate the fact that the nihilist outlook had been correct all along: now the pillars of the world were indeed being shaken, and all the old ways seemed about to be overturned." [220] Scholem eventually wrote a book, published in French, under the title *Du Frankisme au jacobinisme*, about a would-be heir to leadership of the Frankist sect, one Moses Dobruška, alias Junius Frey, who ended up being sent to the guillotine along with Danton in 1794. [221] Thus the attempt by Nerval to examine the Kabbalist sources of French "revolutionary mysticism" by way of the activities of Cagliostro, if pursued with any rigor, would have brought him to the embattled sect of the Sabbatians.

For Scholem, we have seen, one of the more remarkable aspects of Sabbatai Zevi was his sheer ordinariness or "weakness." "There are no unforgettable 'words of the master,' no 'logia,' and nobody seems to have expected any." [222] It is in this context that we would attach weight to Carlyle's remarks on Cagliostro, who, despite his redemptive pretensions, "could not speak; only babble in long-winded diffusions, chaotic circumvolutions tending nowhither. He had no thought for speaking with; he had not even a language."²²³ A common colorlessness seems to have characterized both the upstart count and the savior of the Sabbatians.

Part of the mummery of Cagliostro's Masonic ritual, Benjamin informs us, consisted in his approaching his throne through an honor guard, a "steel arch" formed by the leading adepts of the order, crossing sabres over his head.²²⁴ Thus the would-be "redeemer," promising to conduct his flock, according to Carlyle, "to *perfection* by means of a *physical and moral regeneration*," sounded his messianic call from beneath an arch of steel.²²⁵ For the reader of Benjamin, the idea of waxing messianic beneath a "steel arch" seems a patent recall (or anticipation) of that *apokatastasis* or resurrection of the dead and "entry of souls into Paradise" envisioned at the most profound level of the Arcades Project.²²⁶ (That Benjamin's phrase for what Carlyle calls the "Steel-Arch" is *Stahlstrasse*, a road of steel, does not weaken the point, both because the reality of the arch is described by Benjamin and because the *chemin de fer*, in any event, is amply thematized by Benjamin as connected to the Arcades.) But this is tantamount to saying that Cagliostro, the central figure of the radio script, mediates a relation between Benjamin's inspiration in the Arcades Project and Scholem's thought on Sabbatianism. And he does so even as he binds the two series with which we began our reading of the radio scripts—one on fraud, the other on catastrophe—as no other figure in *Aufklärung für Kinder* does.²²⁷ Carlyle again is of service here. For in characterizing the world of Cagliostro as both a "Workshop and Fancy-Bazaar" and a "Mystic Temple and Hall of Doom," he nicely evokes the world (of fraud or "Fancy-Bazaar" and catastrophe or "Doom") with which we have been concerned in these pages.²²⁸

Might Benjamin himself have intuited the nodality of his Cagliostro script? An answer may be supplied by way of the piece's relation to Goethe. One of the pedagogical touches in *Aufklärung für Kinder* lay in its suggestions for reading to its young audience. Thus the script on "robber bands in old Germany" inevitably adduces the case of Karl Moor in Schiller's tragedy,

Die Räuber.[229] More often than not, however, and for the best pedagogical reasons, Benjamin's suggested reading is Goethe. A passage from *Faust* is inevitably reproduced in "Dr. Faust," and a script on Gypsies ends by recommending the "uncanny, melancholic, and savage 'Zigeunerlied'" to be found among his poems.[230] Now "Cagliostro" is among the scripts that quote from Goethe. Reference is made to the rather overwrought play "Der Grosskophta," in which Cagliostro's infamous role in the Diamond Necklace affair, just prior to the French Revolution, is rehearsed. But Benjamin, like Carlyle, is more intrigued with an episode reported in the *Italiänische Reise*, in which, in Benjamin's words, Goethe "passed himself off as Cagliostro [*Goethe selbst einmal den Cagliostro gespielt hat*]."[231] The anecdote concerns a visit by the poet to Palermo, where he learns that the "Count"'s family is living in poverty. Fascinated by the saga of the "scoundrel-genius," he claims, through an intermediary, to be acquainted with him and to bring the family news of his recent release from the Bastille. Two (rather sentimental) meetings are arranged, during with Goethe learns of unpaid debts to the family by the high-living and notorious "Count." Upon returning to Weimar, he sends the family a significant sum of money, pretending that it came from Cagliostro himself. Thus did the great poet, partially out of "remorse" for his own deception, "pass himself off as Cagliostro." Unless, of course, he were passing himself off as—or becoming—one of Cagliostro's dupes: he had, after all, lost a significant sum in the process. Whatever the case, the luring—to the point of *identification*—of Goethe, that standard of Olympian probity, into the duplicitous world of the pseudo-count gives some sense of the strength exercised by what we have earlier, with Carlyle, called Cagliostro's "weakness" among the radio scripts of *Aufklärung für Kinder*.

Beyond the series concerned with fraud and catastrophe in Benjamin's radio scripts for children, there is a third grouping or series, of somewhat different status, that we have not yet mentioned. For during the initial period that he worked for the Berlin Funkstunde, our author labored—and occasionally chafed—under the additional constraint of being obliged to have a local Berlin focus for his broadcasts. We are thus, for example, treated to excurses on Berlin dialect, on visits to a brass factory and the Borsig machine-works plant, and on Theodor Fontane's *Wanderungen durch die Mark Brandenbourg*.[232] This somewhat artificial restriction no doubt inhibited Benjamin's discursive freedom. Yet simultaneously, it brought his comments in closer proximity to what would eventually take shape as the small masterwork *Eine Berliner Kindheit um 1900*, as well as to Benjamin's own embryonic version of that work, *Berliner Chronik*, which was no doubt already under way during the period he was working for the Berlin radio. To the extent, moreover, as we remarked earlier, that the dream-web of what might be called Benjamin's "unconscious" tended to be cast preferentially less on the human body, as was the case with Freud, than over the topography of a city, it may be suspected that whatever psychoanalytic resonances these radio "sessions" may bear will be compounded rather than impeded by the Berlin-bound restriction.

Consider in this light the script entitled "Das dämonische Berlin."[233] It is devoted to the author's recollections of his childhood relation to the tales of E. T. A. Hoffmann, and is thus in thematic contact with the fragment of *Berliner Kindheit* entitled "Cabinets." In the script, Benjamin evokes his experience at age fourteen, away at school, as a member of a reading group with a special fondness for the tales of Hoffmann. The faculty adviser to the club, who encourages the reading of Hoffman, on one occasion tells his charges: "Very soon [*nächstens*], I shall explain to you to what end [*wozu*] this type of story is written."[234] Benjamin comments: "I am still waiting for that imminent occasion [*nächstens*], and since the worthy man has died in the interim, the explication will have to come to me, if it be at all possible, through such uncanny channels [*auf so unheimliche Weise*], that I prefer to precipitate things a bit and keep, for your benefit, a promise which was made to me many years ago." The imperative to communicate—"uncannily"—to another a crucial message that was in fact never communicated to oneself is a reasonably satisfactory approximation of what transpires in a psychoanalysis, and it is perhaps that reality which has Benjamin, in his script, delving still further into the history of his relations with Hoffman's work.

Thus we are told that in his childhood his parents had denied young Walter permission to read Hoffmann, a circumstance which did not prevent him from secretly perusing his works: "I was supposed to read Hoffman in secret [*nur heimlich*], in the evening, when my parents had gone out. I remember one evening, when I was reading 'The Mines of Falun,' seated alone at the immense dining room table—it was still on Carmerstrasse—in a perfectly silent house, and little by little all the terrors, like so many flat-mouthed fish, emerged from the darkness to gather at the corners of the table, forcing my gaze to fix upon the page as though it were an island of salvation [*eine rettende Insel*], whereas it was the source of all my fears." [235] On another occasion he was so fearful of being caught that he did not understand a single word of the story he was reading (*dass ich kein Wort von der ganzen Geschichte begriffen habe*). [236] That last notation is taken up in slightly modified form in *Eine Berliner Kindheit*, where we read: "I understood nothing of what I was reading. Yet the terrors provoked by every spectral voice, every stroke of midnight, and every malediction multiplied and were realized thanks to the anxieties of an ear permanently attentive to the jingling of the apartment key and the dull shock of my father's cane falling outside into the umbrella rack." [237] Thus whereas the radio script implies that because young Walter was so distracted by his fear he understood nothing, the finished piece on his Berlin childhood suggests that his fear of being caught was ample aesthetic compensation for whatever of the story's contents he was unable to grasp. And indeed a story such as "The Mines of Falun," with its terrified youth and its giant subterranean "father," is so heavily Oedipal as to sustain Benjamin's piquant observation: there may indeed have been not much more to be wrested from the story than a disabling panic in the face of paternal wrath. To have failed, out of disabling Oedipal fear, to penetrate to the story's "inner" meaning is in effect to have penetrated that very interior. The interpretation is enforced by the context in which the episode is placed, a section entitled "Cabinets [*Schränke*]." For its subject is the pleasures and frustrations of penetrating secret recesses. Just prior to an evocation of the forbidden Hoffmann volume locked up in a cabinet, Benjamin recounts his delight, as a child, in plunging his hand into a ball of woolen socks and extracting the one "inside": "I tugged it a bit toward myself, until the phenomenon which plunged me into consternation had occurred: the 'inside sock' had indeed been entirely unrolled and taken out of the purse, but that purse was no longer there. It was impossible for me to experience that enigmatic truth often enough: form and content, the container and the contained, the 'inside sock' and the purse were one and the same thing. A single thing and a third one as well, the result of their metamorphosis."[238] The outer sock *was* the inner one even as the fear that prevented one from understanding or attending to the Hoffmann tale already was an understanding of what was at stake in it.

In the radio script on Hoffmann and "demonic" Berlin, Benjamin will proceed to speculate that the "end" (*wozu*) to which Hoffmann's narrative art tends is an art of "physiognomy," deducing (inner) destiny or character from (outer) gesture or physical shape. But it is surely the paradoxical or disorienting reading of the relations between interiority and exteriority (in *Berliner Kindheit*) which is the richest fruit of Benjamin's encounter with Hoffmann. It is a reading, moreover, which will guide us in our treatment of the next two radio scripts on Berlin to which we shall attend, "Ein Berliner Strassenjunge" and "Mietskaserne."[239]

The first of these is structured, we are told, as the discursive equivalent of "parquetry," replete with three "inlaid motifs or scenes [*eingelegten Bilder und Szenen*]" of choice.[240] The script itself is built around the memoirs of Ludwig Rellstab, a Berlin music critic of the last century. As such it constitutes something of a *Berliner Kindheit* in itself, and it is no surprise that it should deal with places touched on by Benjamin himself in his chronicles of childhood. Witness the first of the three "inlays" in the script. Following an evocation of Rellstab's description of the Berlin Tiergarten, along with an expression of amazement at just how "incredibly" rustic much of it remained at the time of Rellstab's childhood, Benjamin opts to quote from his "friend Franz Hessel"'s work, *Spazieren in Berlin*, on *his* childhood, eighty years later, in the same Berlin park: "All things considered, in the outmoded penumbra of the present, it has remained as overgrown with bushes and as disorienting as thirty or forty years ago, before the Kaiser transformed the natural park into a more untrammeled and presentable place. . . ."[241] Hessel, of course, was one of the tutelary presences of the *Berliner Chronik*: "And then the fifth guide: Franz Hessel. I am not thinking of his book *Spazieren in Berlin*, which was written later, but of that *Nachfeier* accorded our mutual strolls in Paris, this time in the city of our birth, as in a port whose jetty still rises and sinks like a wave beneath the steps of sailors on a ramble."[242] It was with Hessel, Benjamin continues, that he would elaborate a "mythology of the Tiergarten," the necessary prolegomenon to any "doctrine" of the city. These remarks make it clear that Berlin was for Benjamin an "after-feast" or reinscription of Paris. The Berlin Benjamin learned to navigate and dream with Hessel was a displacement, after the fact, of an experience more originarily Parisian.

The second of Benjamin's discursive "inlays" follows a discussion of young Rellstab's fascination with the world of magic and consists largely of a bibliographical recommendation to his young radio audience: a volume demonstrating the performance of magic tricks, Ottokar Fischer's *Das Wunderbuch der Zauberkunst*. Benjamin writes: "A glance at the table of contents will move you to tears, so many tricks does it contain. Don't be afraid of no longer appreciating magic shows after all the explanations. On the contrary: he who knows how to observe attentively, without allowing himself to be taken in by the adroit comments of the prestidigitator and without losing sight of what counts—he alone knows that their incredible skill, their agility, the fruit of training and of zeal, smacks of sorcery [*Hexerei*]."[243] With the world of prestidigitation, we are, of course, in familiar territory, for the "fraud" series of radio scripts with which we began is plainly in resonance with the theme of magic. Benjamin's commentary, moreover, echoes the structure of a text we previously superimposed on the "Teezug" sequence, the short story "Rastelli erzählt . . ." For just as that tale (of a fraudulent master juggler) concludes with the shocking revelation that the juggler's "unbelievable" command performance was indeed "unbelievable" (since the dwarf, the juggler's accomplice in fraud, had not shown up), so in the commentary just cited, the demystification of the magician's performance opens onto a still greater vista of mystification (or "sorcery"). The result, in brief, of this second "inlay" is to inscribe "Ein Berliner Strassenjunge" in the series of scripts concerned with "fraud."

The third "inlay" brings us to one of the recurrent motifs of the *Berliner Chronik*, labyrinths. Having referred to the cover of a Rellstab volume which depicts the section of the Tiergarten in which he had encountered his first labyrinth, Benjamin proceeds, at the end of what he calls his "labyrinthine" broadcast, to recommend an exhibition of labyrinths currently on display in Berlin. The dream of labyrinths, however, was a dream, we read in *Berliner Chronik*, first satisfied in Paris: "Paris taught me that art of losing oneself; it satisfied that dream whose most archaic trace is the labyrinth drawn on the blotter paper of my school notebooks."[244] Moreover, later in the same text, Benjamin recalls a "violent" desire, which seized him in Paris, in the Café des Deux Magots, to schematize in diagrammatic form his own life. The result was what he calls a "labyrinth" of "originary relations," inscribed on a sheet of paper he was to lose a year or two thereafter, but which continued to haunt him.[245] Thus the link between Paris and labyrinths echoes the relation in the earlier "inlay," established by way of the allusion to Hessel, between Paris and Berlin. Behind Berlin, in both cases, we find a phantasm of Paris. That bit of trickery, moreover, is a feature of a script whose placement in the series concerned with "fraud" we have established.

Within the Berlin series, and directly opposite the "labyrinthine" script on "fraud" (or "prestidigitation"), we find a script whose subject is "catastrophe." Its title is "Die Mietskaserne," which means "tenement house" or more literally: "rental barracks." Its subject is the development whereby Berlin itself became the "largest 'rental barracks' in the world," and the merit of the struggle, since 1925, against that sorry state of affairs.[246] The phenomenon, we are told, is linked to Berlin's traditional status as a military or garrison city. The harshness of Prussian military life was such that soldiers tended to desert. Frederic the Great's solution was to house soldiers' families with them in collective barracks in Berlin, thereby depriving them of any refuge to which to desert. Thus the civilian population itself, in its living arrangements, became effectively militarized: the age of "rental barracks" (or apartment blocks) had begun. What made things worse was Frederic's decision to build upward rather than outward. "Paris was his model [*Vorbild*]."[247] This, Benjamin explains, was an unjustifiable error: "Paris was a fortified city, unable to expand beyond the zone of fortifications and bastions. With its 150,000 inhabitants, it was the largest in Europe, and Parisians had to resolve to build houses of several stories. Berlin was never a fortified city. . . . Thus nothing prevented the city from expanding on the ground."[248] Thus even as the labyrinths of Berlin, exhilarating exercises in the complication of horizontality, were only secondarily German for Benjamin (in the previously discussed script), so, in "Die Mietskaserne," is the "rental barracks," a depressingly "monumental and solemn" simplification of verticality, primarily French.[249] In both cases—labyrinths and "barracks"—a quintessential and almost "mythological" dimension of Berlin turns out to be falsely originary, a displacement or borrowing from Paris. Which is to say that both labyrinth and barracks appear to be caught up in an experience of disorientation for which we are hard put to find a better word than "labyrinthine." The opposition between barracks (*Kaserne*) and labyrinth would appear, in brief, to be in the order of an illusion generated by the labyrinth itself.

Several years later, in Paris, Georges Bataille, whom Benjamin saw with some regularity at sessions of the Collège de Sociologie, would develop something of an (anti-)metaphysics identical in structure to the configuration whose lineaments we have just derived from the Berlin radio scripts. Disorienting horizontality, which Bataille termed "labyrinthine," figured a frenzy for communication in which being itself was squandered.[250] The vertical instance of command, hierarchy, or control (corresponding to Benjamin's high-rise "barracks") he thematized as a "pyramid." Thus Bataille: "The flight oriented toward the summit (which is, dominating knowledge itself, the organization of knowledge) is only one of the itineraries of the 'labyrinth.' But that itinerary, which we must follow from illusion [*leurre*] to illusion in quest of 'being,' can in no way be avoided."[251] Denis Hollier comments that the pyramid is thus a product of the labyrinth itself, or rather that the opposition between the pyramid and the labyrinth is not quite tenable.[252] It is a conclusion identical to our own concerning the relation between the two "originary" Berlin formations in Benjamin's radio scripts, and one that encourages speculation as to just what the tenor of the communications between Benjamin and Bataille was—or might have been—during the immediate prewar years in Paris.[253]

The "barracks" of Berlin's urban renewal seems like the reverse of the "barricades" against whose possibility the urban renewal of Paris, undertaken by Haussmann, and lamented in the Arcades Exposé, was undertaken. For Benjamin, Haussmann's "strategic beautification" of the city, with its rapid rise in rents and destruction of old neighborhoods, was a catastrophe of biblical dimensions. As the first Arcades Exposé puts it: "*Les Jérémiades d'un haussmannisé* (an anonymous tract of 1868) gives [the reaction of a displaced citizen] the form of a biblical lamentation."[254] The urban renewal of Berlin—consecrating the era of the "rental barracks"—is also characterized as a "catastrophe." Here is the development culminating in that conclusion: "It turned out that a number of the roads envisaged traversed private property. The state, the initiator of the plan, should have compensated the landowners. That would have been quite expensive inasmuch as there was not yet a law of eminent domain. In order to build roads without any significant outlay of cash, the state had to win over the landowners. And a few sly functionaries thought: we shall authorize them to build in such manner that their rents give them more income than they would have received from the sale of the plots we need. And that ruse provoked the catastrophe [*das grösste Unglück*]. . . ."²⁵⁵ The state would compensate landowners for whatever loss they might incur from land needed for the construction of roads by irresponsibly authorizing the building (and renting) of higher housing units. The "catastrophe," that is, is inseparable in this case from an instance of corruption or fraud. But the inseparability—or "translatability"—of fraud and catastrophe has been the focus of our reading of the radio scripts from the beginning. Indeed, we approached "Die Mietskaserne" itself, by way of the Parisian "model" on which it draws, as a translation of "Ein Berliner Strassenjunge," a script about labyrinths and "prestidigitation" (or fraud), which, for all its appeal to original experiences, seemed similarly constituted as a post-Parisian *Nachfeier* (or "after-feast").

The mutual permeability of "fraudulence" and "catastrophe," though, brought us to the motif of the "false messiah," and, by way of Scholem, to the legacy of Sabbatian antinomianism. At the center of that tradition lay the notion of a "commandment to be fulfilled by means of a transgression [*mitzvah ha-ba'ah ba-averah*]."²⁵⁶ But in the present context—(horizontal) "labyrinth" and (vertical) "barracks" resurfacing, in their odd entanglement, as "labyrinth" and "pyramid" in Bataille—does not the Sabbatian precept appear to anticipate what is perhaps the central affirmation of Bataille's *L'Erotisme*: "Transgression is not the negation of a prohibition [*interdit*], but its completion and transcendence."²⁵⁷ Such would be the initial (and by no means negligible) interpretive payoff of the reading of Benjamin with Bataille prompted by our analysis of "Ein Berliner Strassenjunge" and "Die Mietskaserne."

Among the more revealing of the Berlin scripts is a two-part excursus, containing material that will surface in the Arcades Project, "Berliner Spielzeugwanderung."[258] It is a reflection on the changing world of children's toys but is most interesting in its framing conceit. Benjamin recounts a fairy tale, "Schwester Tinchen," known to his audience from a popular anthology. The story tells of an impoverished family of four boys and a girl who are told by a fairy godmother that she will always protect them so long as they get on well together. An evil magician arrives with numerous gifts and promptly provokes strife among the boys by casting the gifts in their midst. Because they have fought, the boys are taken away in a sack by the magician's attendant devils. Only the girl, Tinchen, who was not party to the fray, is spared, and it now befalls her to undergo an ordeal which will allow her to save her brothers: "Only one thing is asked of her . . . : not to stop, not even for an instant, in her journey through the land of the evil magician, not until she arrives at his cavern. The magician, to prevent her from succeeding, will try to retain her through chimerical images [*Gaukelbildern*]. Should she cry out even once: 'I want to stay here [*Hier will ich bleiben*],' she will fall under his power."[259] Tinchen, then, as Benjamin subsequently comments, is Faust as a little girl, challenged to utter the child's equivalent of "Verweile doch, du bist so schön." The evil magician's trump card, however, is that he disposes of an infinite variety of irresistible toys, which have Tinchen perpetually on the brink of succumbing to his lures.

In the course of the script, which would ideally bring Tinchen and her brothers back home, the destination of her travels undergoes a change. In Benjamin's words: "She traversed several kingdoms. . . . We might follow her step by step if this program were not called 'The Berlin Hour [*die Berlinstunde*],' and if I were not obliged, while Tinchen is in the land of magic [*im Zauberland*], to return to Berlin via mysterious underground paths."[260] Thus the protagonist's perilous voyage back home has been displaced into the narrator's passage to Berlin. Benjamin drops the subject of the brothers awaiting their salvation, and proceeds to forge a metaphor whereby the enchanted land strewn with irresistible toys finds it equivalent in the department stores of downtown Berlin: "You're in a rush to get to Berlin, but I'm already there. For what I have told you about the enchanted land the girl has to cross through bravely without tarrying I could as well have told you about the commercial galleries of Berlin, which you have all crossed through bravely without tarrying. And sometimes, when your mother had time, while tarrying. You see what I'm getting at, I think; you know where to find those long galleries of toys [*Spielzeuggalerien*] without either fairy or magician. In department stores."[261] Whereupon the rest of the broadcast and most of the following one are spent evoking the charms of the various toys presently—and formerly—available in (unnamed) Berlin stores. Benjamin, that is, casts himself in the role of a Tinchen, who forgets the imperative of saving her "brothers." Or worse yet, in that of the "evil magician," since it is he who seems to be exciting the desires of the children of Berlin for the merchandise he describes. He even anticipates an "avalanche" of letters from distraught parents on that score, and seems singularly unprepared to answer them (*Was soll ich dann darauf antworten?*).

It is difficult to read of the "enchanted land" of the evil magician and its counterpart, the "enchanted" galleries of Berlin department stores without being reminded of Benjamin's comments on the "fetishization" of merchandise in the Arcades Exposés. The "universal expositions" of Paris, in which that fetishization was consecrated, "inaugurate a phantasmagoria which man enters for his own entertainment."[262] An extended—and more adult—version of the Tinchen tale, moreover, made its way into the highly wrought prose of one of the early drafts for the Arcades Project: "When Hackländer, in one of his tales, made use of the entirely new invention of the luxury industry, he too placed fantastic dolls in the dangerous gallery Tinchen had to transverse, on order of the fairy Concordia, in order to free her poor brothers." Benjamin then quotes at length a passage from the tale in which Tinchen appears about to succumb to the charms of a magnificent doll. Whereupon: "The child may no longer want to hear toys that speak, but the maleficent spell of that perilous pass may still—even today—take the form of huge dolls, moving to and fro. But who today still remembers the site where women, during the last decades of the past century, offered men their most seductive aspect, promised them, with utmost intimacy, their very silhouette? In those asphalt-covered indoor spaces in which bicycling was taught. The female cyclist disputes pride of place with the 'chansonette' as a subject for Chéret's posters and gives fashion its most daring line."[263] Sexual dalliance, in the Arcades draft, has taken the place of ogling merchandise, in the radio script, as the substance of what is allegorized in the enchanted land of the tale. The difference, moreover, is not crucial, since fashion, a phenomenon essential to the "cult of merchandise," according to the Arcades Exposé, has always had as its central feature the imparting of "sex appeal to the inorganic."[264] What both versions have in common is a forgetting of their assumed end, the rescue of the forlorn brothers. But if the enchanted land or gallery of merchandise is indeed at some level an allegorization of the Arcades, then Benjamin's twofold truncation of the tale begins to assume broader significance. For it is as though the investment in the arcades were at some level an investment in the Arcades Project itself. At which point the story, in Benjamin's truncated version, would seem to convey an allegory of what Scholem, in his biography, called the "severe and finally irreconcilable competition" between the pursuit of the Arcades Project and the resumption of his Hebrew studies.[265]

Or consider a further version of what appears to be at stake less in the Tinchen tale than in Benjamin's willful straying from its intended end: the section of *Berliner Kindheit*—to which we have already referred—entitled "Sexual Awakening":

> It was in one of the streets that I later frequented by night, wandering without end, that I was surprised, when the time came, by an awakening of sexual desire, and that in the strangest circumstances. It was during the Jewish New Year, and my parents had made arrangements to have me admitted to some religious ceremony. It was probably with the reformed community, for which my mother, out of family tradition, felt some sympathy, whereas orthodox ritual was from birth familiar to my father. But he had to yield. I was entrusted for the day to the care of a distant relative, whom I was to meet at his home. But either because I lost his address, or because I lost my way in his neighborhood, it got later and later, and my wandering became increasingly desperate. There could be no question of my going to the synagogue on my own, since my guardian had the entrance tickets. The reason for my misfortune should be ascribed to my indifference toward the virtually unknown relative assigned me and to my mistrust of religious ceremonies, which seemed to promise only embarrassment and discomfort. In my state of total disarray, of a sudden, a burning wave of anxiety invaded me—"too late, it's all over for the synagogue"—and before it could recede, at exactly the same moment, another came, this time one of perfect insouciance—"come what may, I don't give a damn." And those two waves fused their energies irresistibly in a first great experience of pleasure: the violation of the holiday united with the procuring street, which made me anticipate for the first time the services with which it was to supply adult desire.[266]

In relation to the Tinchen tale, the enchanted land or gallery has become the *flâneur's* street, and, more interestingly, the mission of saving the "brothers" has become a high holiday visit to the synagogue. But whereas the rescue mission seems merely forgotten or overlooked by Benjamin in the use he makes of the tale, the failure to visit the synagogue, experienced as a "profanation" of the holy day, becomes central to the sexual life inaugurated, after the fact, by this episode. That significantly deferred genesis of sexual fantasy per se of necessity took the form of what Freud called "wish-fulfillment." And yet at the same time it appears so patently to prefigure what is by general agreement the failure or tragedy of Benjamin's life as to raise the question of what indeed may have been "fulfilled" by that failure. For in the economy of Benjamin's life one is hard put not to superimpose the lingering in Paris, in pursuit of the uncompleted Arcades Project, "theater of all my struggles and all my ideas," on the loitering in the "procuring street." Even as one is inclined to see in the need for a patron to escort him to the synagogue and the ultimate avoidance of attending the service prefigurations of his failure to make the much anticipated trip (under Scholem's patronage) to Palestine. The resonances between the fragment from *Berliner Kindheit* and the shape of Benjamin's life, that is, make of "Sexual Awakening" one of those passages, in the words of the same book, which "that invisible stranger, the Future, appears to have forgotten in our midst." [267] Unless, of course, the fragment be one of those "wishes," mentioned by Benjamin a few pages before, whose subsequent fulfillment in the course of one's life one fails to recognize . . . [268]

Let us review the three sets of relations—in apparent violation of any distinction between Benjamin's life and work—which we have just superimposed. On the one hand: Tinchen's wandering in the enchanted land of the evil genius; its homologue, the phantasmagoria attaching to merchandise in the shopping "galleries" of Berlin; the Arcades Project per se; the attraction of the (sexually) "procuring street"; and the ultimately tragic decision to remain in Paris as war approached. On the other: the forgetting (by Benjamin if not Tinchen) of the mission to save the "brothers"; the abandoned study of Hebrew; the "profanation" of the high holy day (in "Sexual Awakening"); and the deferment of the anticipated trip to Palestine. It is the positivity of that "profanation," we said, which inflects the entire configuration in a new direction. For it situates "sexual awakening" (and its homologues: the Arcades Project, the lingering in Paris) in transgressive counterpoint to the Hebrew series. [269] The point can be sustained by examining one of Benjamin's more hermetic texts, the semiautobiographical fantasia, "Agesilaus Santander." In that posthumously published text, which Scholem has discussed in a justly celebrated essay, the author speaks of his parents' decision to bestow on him "two, further exceptional" names, which he might use in the event he became a writer, since "it would be good if not everybody noticed at once that I was a Jew." [270] The author, however, keeps the name secret, proceeding with it "as did the Jews with the additional name of their children." The reference is to the Hebrew name by which children are called to the Torah upon reaching "maturity." The narrator, in sum, has reversed the parental imperative, and finds himself not a crypto-Jewish writer, as intended by his parents, but a Jew with a secretly "non-Jewish" identity. Or rather, that non-Jewish identity, to the extent that it is modeled on the Jewish custom of assigning "secret" or additional Hebrew names to their children, is, by analogy, both Hebrew and non-Jewish. The name itself, however, "Agesilaus Santander," is interpreted by Scholem as an anagram of *Der Angelus Satan* (the Angel Satan). We are thus, by implication, invited to imagine the unthinkable scenario of the young narrator, upon reaching maturity, being called to the Law under the name of the Angel Satan. Moreover, since "maturity," according to "Agesilaus Santander," "can occur more than once in life" (by which we are to understand, according to Scholem, that one may fall in love several times over), sexual experience itself is intimately caught up in the calling of the Angel Satan to the Law. Whereby we rejoin the "profanatory" impulse behind "Sexual Awakening." But does that reading not also converge with the Sabbatian inspiration which has emerged from our reading of the radio scripts? For what indeed might "Agesilaus Santander" do upon being ritually called to the Law if not, "stepping out of his name," pretend to fulfill it by way of its own violation? [271]

Scholem is eloquent and informative on the Klee painting, *Angelus Novus*, which served as Benjamin's principal source for the figure of the "New Angel" in "Agesilaus Santander." Moreover, he situates the Kabbalistic reference in the text, and traces its vicissitudes in Benjamin's later writings. Of particular interest in the present context is his observation that "the Luciferian element entered Benjamin's meditations on Klee's picture not directly from the Jewish tradition, but rather from the occupation with Baudelaire that fascinated him for so many years."[272] For that comment recalls the role of Paris (and French culture generally) in the homology we have been constructing: its superimposability on the enchanted land of the Tinchen tale, the world of the arcades, the Arcades Project itself, and the "procuring street." If the Sabbatian call to fulfill the Law by violating it is based on a putative mission to defeat "evil" from within, and if our ultimate image of Benjamin has him waxing desperately messianic amid a fantasia of the arcades of nineteenth-century Paris, does not (anti-Semitic) France itself come to occupy that exile— or "evil"—within which the Sabbatian is called on to exercise his transgressive calling?

Consider, for example, one of the first comments Benjamin feels impelled to make in the first section ("La Bohème") of his Baudelaire study: "The *culte de la blague*, which may be rediscovered in Georges Sorel and which has become a staple of fascist propaganda, sprouts its first buds in Baudelaire. The title under which (and the spirit in which) Céline wrote his *Bagatelles pour un massacre* refer us immediately to a note in Baudelaire's journal: 'A fine conspiracy to be organized for the extermination of the Jewish race'."[273] One could no doubt organize a short history of French anti-Semitism around Benjamin's defensive statement: from the authoritarian-theological mode inspired by Baudelaire's mentor, de Maistre, to the proto-fascist pre-World War I variety championed briefly by Sorel (but celebrated as the focus of a revival in the 1930s) to the rantings of Céline just prior to the genocide. Indeed one might even add on the name of Gide, whose genteel anti-Semitism took the form, echoed by Benjamin here, of dismissing Céline's call to an anti-Jewish massacre as no more than a "jest [*jeu*]."[274] And with Baudelaire, the subject of Benjamin's ongoing interest; Sorel, whose apocalyptical, anti-"progressive" leftism had left its mark on him as early as "The Critique of Violence"; and Gide, the "principal contemporary," whom he had deferentially interviewed not long before, we are touching on three of the most significant references in Benjamin's France. Thus, although, according to Scholem, Benjamin, at the time, "was under no illusions about the dimensions of anti-Semitism in France," and indeed was capable of giving Scholem several examples of the phenomenon among left-wing French intellectuals which the latter admits to being "ashamed to repeat," we are treated to the disheartening spectacle of Benjamin attempting to disarm Céline's 1938 call to a massacre of the Jews from *within*, as it were, by dismissing it as no more than a joke.[275] Or perhaps Benjamin, here, is best viewed in terms of the text with which we began our reading of the radio scripts for children, the "Teezug" episode. For even as the piquancy of that sequence lay in the fact that the imbibers, to their shock, were served exactly what they ordered ("iced tea"), so the joke (on Benjamin) in this case was precisely that there was no joke: the Jews were effectively served just what they had been promised. That the trains this time were heading east from France, rather than south toward New Orleans, offers no doubt a criterion for establishing what does—or does not—constitute a "children's" tale.

Beyond Baudelaire, Sorel, and Gide, one of the French authors who counted most importantly in Benjamin's later projects was Léon Daudet. For the autobiographical *Berliner Chronik*, as we have seen, makes reference to "an illustrious precursor, the Frenchman Léon Daudet, exemplary at least in the title of his work, which exactly encompasses the best that I might achieve here: *Paris vécu*." [276] Now Daudet, who was arguably the most influential French literary critic of the twentieth century, played a decisive role in securing the Prix Goncourt for Proust, as well as in launching the literary careers of Bernanos and Céline. But he was known above all as an anti-Semitic ideologue: an early collaborator of Edouard Drumont, the journalist and author of *La France juive*, a best-selling "classic" of French anti-Semitism; and a co-founder and editor of *Action française*. Here, for instance, is *Paris vécu*, the book within whose shadow Benjamin would write his life, on the intimate bond between Daudet and

Drumont: "*La France juive* appeared on the stands. . . . Its success was stunning, and it was I, informed by the vendors of the galleries of the Odéon, who came to announce it to the author. Drumont's joy was something to behold . . . we drank to the health of the book that was about to positively revolutionize Paris." [277] Benjamin's phrase concerning the role of "the title at least" of Daudet's book in his own literary project bespeaks the extreme caution with which he would have had to enter a book so jovial at the prospect of his own ejection. Even as the rush to insist on the "joking" quality of Baudelaire's—then Céline's—call to massacre the Jews bespeaks a remarkable reticence to take those authors at their word. "Evil" there might be, but can anyone doubt that such gingerly efforts as these could have little hope—whether from within or without—of disarming it?

Finally, in our miniature gallery of the France from which Benjamin would never emerge, we would adduce a passage from the celebrated text that lay at the inception of the entire Arcades Project, Aragon's *Le Paysan de Paris*. In "Le Passage de l'Opéra" section of that work, Aragon gauges the anger vented by the merchants and denizens of an arcade about to be sacrificed to the commercial aspirations of a realty company located (fittingly) on Boulevard Haussmann. After reproducing a going-out-of-business notice, signed "combattant 1914–1918; wounded veteran," he writes: "This is the first sign we encounter in the arcades of a legitimate agitation which has taken hold of the denizens of the locale since the publication of the compensation estimated by the realty corporation of the City of Paris for public works on the Boulevard Haussmann. There is a veritable civil war going on, which for the moment is restricted to legal maneuvers and taunts, to debates between businessmen and newspapers, but which could, were the exasperation of the victims to increase, take a turn toward barricades and gunshots: there is in these calm shops an accumulated rancor which could result some time next year in a shopkeepers' Fort Chabrol." [278] One may wonder, whether Benjamin—who wrote to Adorno, in 1935, that his initial encounter with the Aragon text had been so intense that he could not read more than two or three pages at a sitting—recognized the "Fort Chabrol" reference.[279] Situated on the rue Chabrol, it was, at the time of the Dreyfus affair, the headquarters of the Ligue antisémite, and the publishing site of the journal *L'Antijuif*. In 1899, following the riots that greeted the death of the president of the Republic, a mandate was issued for the arrest of Jules Guérin, leader of the Ligue. He responded by barricading himself (and his followers) into the "fort," which was then blockaded by the police for more than a month, before Guérin surrendered. "Fort Chabrol," then—the "end of the nineteenth century," as Bernanos called it—was part of the saga of French anti-Semitism.[280] And in Aragon's reading, the "legitimate effervescence" of the displaced victims of the disappearing arcades would quite properly issue in a new "Fort Chabrol." From the time of Drumont's *Mon vieux Paris*, after all, if not before, fidelity to old Paris and fury at its destroyers had been a staple of French anti-Semites. It was, then, we may assume, a considerable challenge for Benjamin to enter the struggle for "reviving" the arcades without ending up in Aragon's "Fort Chabrol."

Perhaps our point might best be encapsulated by recalling an anecdote from Scholem's memoir of his friendship with Benjamin. In 1938, while Benjamin was in Ibiza, Scholem spent several days in Paris and consulted his friend about lodging. "For my days in Paris, Benjamin initially suggested that I stay with his sister, or, if that could not be arranged, that I go to the Hôtel Littré, not far from the rue de Rennes, where he was well known. How great was my surprise when it turned out that we had landed in a hotbed of French fascism, where the concierge and quite a few of the guests gave us strange looks and the only available paper was the *Action Française*. It has remained a mystery to me how Benjamin could have steered us there." [281] The France into which Benjamin had plunged, the France of Sorel, Daudet, and the future "Fort Chabrol" of the Arcades, finds its emblem in the Hôtel Littré, "hotbed of French fascism." The Sabbatian mandate to enter into evil—*for whatever reason*—had been fulfilled, and it is particularly ironic that Scholem, Benjamin's initiator in the subject, should have failed to grasp the desperate lesson his friend, we may assume, was imparting to him.

Were one to secularize the Sabbatian imperative (were, that is, Sabbatianism not in itself a mode of secularization), one would quickly arrive at the vexed topos of "Jewish self-hatred." For the Jewish anti-Jewish thrust of the call to "fulfill the Law by violating it" *could* be interpreted as little else. In Benjamin's own work, the text which of necessity is most concerned with that motif is the essay on Karl Kraus, the great Viennese satirist who converted to Catholicism and whom Benjamin compared to Léon Bloy.[282] The essay on Kraus, moreover, is of particular pertinence in this context in that the "New Angel" of "Agesilaus Santander" passes significantly through it. In his will to make of language a figuration of apocalypse, the author of *The Last Days of Mankind* becomes for Benjamin an avenging angel. "Perhaps one of those who, according to the Talmud, are at each moment created anew in countless throngs, and who, once they have raised their voices before God, cease and pass into nothingness."[283] Just so the "New Angel" of "Agesilaus Santander," where the identical tradition is ascribed to Kabbalah.[284] On the subject of (Jewish) anti-Semitism, Benjamin quotes approvingly Kraus's witticism: "Anti-Semitism is the mentality . . . that means seriously a tenth part of the jibes that the stock-exchange wit holds ready for his own blood."[285] The remark suggests both that anti-Semitism is a restrictive misinterpretation of Jewish self-hatred, but that Jewish self-hatred is in itself more in the order of a *Witz* (or "jibe") than anything else. The remark is precious in that it authorizes an articulation between Benjamin and Freud on this issue. For Freud "primary masochism" informs the economy of the unconscious, and sadism figures at best a restrictive (or egological) economy within it. Freud's "primary masochism," that is, is to Kraus's (or Benjamin's) "Jewish self-hatred" as the former's sadism is to the latter's (latters'?) anti-Semitism. That the opposition between the two economies in Kraus (and Benjamin) is that between the joke and the "serious," moreover, allows one to superimpose still again the division in Kraus's formulation on that in Freud's: the Freudian *Witz*, after all, is informed by the same triangularity in its genesis as the unconscious "drive."[286] In sum, if a certain ludic or *witzig* reading of "Jewish self-hatred" in (Benjamin's) Kraus—perhaps the stuff of what Freud called "Jewish humor"—can be superimposed on what Freud termed "primary masochism," the continuity between our own "Sabbatian" reading of Benjamin and, say, Laplanche's reading of Freud would be established.

Apokatastasis: the final (failed) image of the "weak" messiah of the Paris Arcades, patiently collecting the wherewithal to effect a general resurrection and "entry into Paradise," is among the most gripping in the history of twentieth-century criticism. Of the figures in Benjamin's thought, moreover, who best emblematize that messianic undertaking, surely the Baudelairean *chiffonnier*, the ragpicker bent on glory, deserves what one hesitates to call pride of place. For the Messiah too is a collector, a scavenger among the refuse of history, and ultimately the leader of a "cortège of the vanquished."[287]

To the list of *chiffonniers*, Benjamin added the figure of Croniamental, the poet become ragpicker of Apollinaire's *Le poète assassiné*. Adorno's contribution, in a critical letter of 10 November 1938, was the *chiffonnier* of Charpentier's *Louise:* "the dark source of light of an entire opera."[288] Our own addition bears particularly on Benjamin's case both because it manages to associate the figure of the ragpicker with an Edenic resurrection and because it comes from one of Benjamin's preferred authors. In a letter from Paris of 5 June 1927 to Hofmannsthal, Benjamin singled out "Giraudoux and Aragon above all" as the French authors for whom he felt an affinity.[289] Imagine then an implausible hybrid of the two French authors. The embittered "*expropriés de demain*" of Aragon's arcade, already intuiting the demolition of their world, make a plea to the banks: let the shopowners of the arcade hold on to their businesses just long enough to profit from the upcoming Grand Exposition. Aragon: "One allows them to hope for the delay they request, and the Exposition, which throughout most of the country scarcely excites anyone, here appears as the Redemptress [*Rédemptrice*], the new sun that it had been for the men of 1888 and 1889."[290] Enter Jean Giraudoux, who, after a slight displacement of neighborhood, gives the disgruntled Parisians a true *Rédemptrice*, under the name of the "Folle de Chaillot." For it is her success in doing away with the speculators about to expropriate her small band of Parisian neighborhood zanies that is celebrated in his famous play of 1944.

Concerning Giraudoux's work, several aspects are of particular interest in the current context.[291] No sooner does the Madwoman lure the speculators to their collective (underground) doom than a massive resurrection takes place. A wall opens up on the set and several "cortèges" file on stage. The leader of the first group speaks: "Thank you, Countess. As compensation for your subterranean dispatches, we have at last been freed. We are those who have saved animal races. This is Jean Cornell, who saved the beaver; and this, the Baron de Blérancourt, who saved the Saint-Germain hound. . . ."[292] The head of the second cohort of the resurrected thanks the Madwoman for her "relève," then goes on to identify his troop as consisting of those who have saved or created a plant. The names—Pasteur, Jussieu—are again as strikingly French as in the first group. The atmosphere, with its rare species and the pleasure of naming them, is plainly Edenic, and the more Gallic the more Edenic it is. Now the Madwoman's leading male associate (and the male star of the play) is *Le Chiffonnier*. It is he who, in the play, identifies the source of the malaise rampant in the Madwoman's community: the arrival in Paris of a "different race"—of speculators—intent on despoiling the very air that one breathes.[293] Now it is not our intention to rehearse in this context the anti-Semitic underpinnings of the *Chiffonnier's* line, as it was written for performance in Nazi-occupied Paris. It would entail a reading of what Scholem himself calls the "downright Streicherian tones" of the anti-Semitic passages of *Pleins pouvoirs* (1939), as well as tracing the transitions in Giraudoux's work whereby Moïse, the quintessential Jew of *Eglantine* (1927), becomes the "President" or latter-day King Solomon of *Cantiques des cantiques* (1938), before metamorphosing into the "President" of the doomed cartel of speculators in *La Folle de Chaillot*.[294] Perhaps the point can be brought home most forcefully by comparing the achievement of those deserving resurrection at the end of *La Folle de Chaillot* (saving from extinction a single species of plant or animal) with the contents of a scene, ultimately cut, from Giraudoux's first play, *Siegfried*, in which Zelten, a surrogate for the author, declines, during a time of political turmoil, to spare from the death penalty the last surviving speaker of a particularly poetic dialect of Yiddish.[295]

By the cruelest of ironies, when the resurrection finally came to France, heralded by a *chiffonnier*, it was, a few years after Benjamin's death, in the form of an allegory of the genocide of the Jews. Might he have dreamed as much? *Chiffonnier* translates into German as *Lumpensammler*—a collector of rags, but also of scoundrels. And the preeminent "collector" of *Lumpen* in world history was Louis Napoleon, as evoked by Marx in *The Eighteenth Brumaire of Louis Bonaparte*. When Hannah Arendt, moreover, attempted an analytic history of the Dreyfus affair, she could do no better than project Marx's scheme in that work onto *fin de siècle* France: the anti-Semitic "mob" for Bonaparte's *Lumpen* cohort, and Jules Guérin (of Fort Chabrol) in the role of Bonaparte himself.[296] So that the "Fort Chabrol" of the Arcades predicted by Aragon in the text whose consequences for Benjamin were so decisive may ultimately have been staged—and above all may have triumphed—in the play by Giraudoux. As our texts—by Aragon, Benjamin, and Giraudoux—merge with historical reality, as the apocatastasis of Benjamin's *chiffonnier* gives way to the resurrection witnessed by Giraudoux's, it is difficult to imagine a more devastating enactment of the messianic dream of plunging into evil, albeit to defeat it from within.

That such a configuration—"mosaic" or "anti-Mosaic," as one likes—can have been generated through a reading of Benjamin's apparently transparent radio scripts is an index of the surprising depths of the thinker as well as of the bitter "enlightenment" that children of all ages, as the cliché goes, may draw from them.

MATURITY

2

(Canis Major: Constellation of the Unconscious)

Toward the end of *Aufklärung für Kinder,* there appears an apparently aberrant script under the title "Wahre Geschichten von Hunden." [1] For it is dominated by neither catastrophe nor fraud nor recollections of the city of Berlin. Here then is a sequence of tales about a boy's putative best friend, and it is to what is at stake in the constellation they form with other such tales, in the context of the collection of scripts they all but conclude that these remarks are devoted.

The script begins with an exercise in what Brecht called "estrangement": a long passage from Linnaeus, characterizing dogs, is reproduced in the thought that the evocation is so "surprising" in its precision that had the word "dog" not been pronounced one would have had a hard time guessing which animal was being described. Linnaeus's dog, then, as reproduced by Benjamin, has something of the uncanny charge of the demonic (or Mephistophelian) "spaniel" evoked by Goethe in a passage from *Faust,* which Benjamin quoted at length in his own script on "Dr. Faust." [2] The dog appears as something familiar but estranged, the issue of an unsettling transformation.

The dog, Benjamin goes on to say, is the only animal (with the possible exception of the horse) with whom humans have established bonds of intimacy. How so? "At the origin of it all lies the great victory, which man carried off, thousands of years ago, over dogs (in fact, over wolves and jackals). It was in becoming de-

83

pendent on man and in allowing themselves to be tamed [*zäh-men*] by him, that those wild animals became dogs." [3] Dog, then, is another name for the master-slave relationship, an abbreviation, as such, for dialectic. [4] And it is here, in fact, that a first step in the direction of the unconscious may be taken. For to the extent that dialectic is above all a dialectic of consciousness, and the dog *qua* dog is repressive of energies that have been excluded in the dialectic of his genesis, the wolf dormant within the dog would appear to afford a figure of the "unconscious." All that dialectic cannot encompass, all that might bring dialectic to a "standstill," stands poised for release in the very being of the dog. [5]

And such returns of the repressed, or relapses into a feral state, Benjamin tells his audience, have been known to occur: "And it is quite regrettable that subsequent to being trained, certain dogs, particularly mastiffs, have lapsed into their former feral state, becoming even more ferocious [*in ihrem Blutdurst schrecklicher wurden*] than originally." [6] Here the telling factor is the supplementary ferocity, beyond any natural quantity, which the return of the repressed carries with it. For such an incremental displacement captures the distinction between (instinctual) aggressiveness and (sexual) sadism, which Laplanche's reading of Freud, among others, has pinpointed as the very locus of the unconscious. [7]

Ultimately, of course, in its median existence between lupine ferocity and human warmth, the dog straddles the line of demarcation between nature (or animality) and culture (humankind). But that boundary, at which Lévi-Strauss locates the prohibition of incest, is for that reason a figure of what he, like Freud, calls the unconscious. Benjamin, who makes no mention of either incest or the unconscious in this script, nonetheless organizes it around the two extremes of animal ferocity and (super-)human devotion which the dog manages to bridge. Thus, if the script details sequences of animal viciousness, at one end, it gradates toward stories of fidelity in mourning at the other. Once again, then, be it through the suggestion of a (master-slave) dialectic

and a "wildness" which that dialectic can but precariously contain, or the supplementary viciousness (or "sadism") of such
wildness when it does return, or, as in the present case, the median situation between "nature" and "culture," Benjamin appears to have produced another maze in which all paths
(mis)lead to the "unconscious."

Consider now the tales of dogs mourning with which Benjamin concludes his script. The first, reminiscent of a Kafka par-
able, tells of a "large black dog" in England who would follow
funeral processions with such disruptive regularity that his very
presence was eventually integrated into the funeral ceremony:
"It was finally decided not to upset the silent mourner, and ever
since he has participated officially in all burials." [8] However familiar a creature the mournful dog became, however, his success
in *anticipating* a death on a steamer arriving in port revives the
uncanniness (*Seltsamkeit*) characterizing the canine from the inception of the script.

The second canine *Trauerspiel* is in fact a long quotation from
Ludwig Börne's volume, *Die Suppe*. It relates the celebrity of
Medor, the "emperor of dogs." [9] Something of a prefiguration of
Benjamin's Baudelaire, Medor was to be found, shortly after the
Revolution of 1830, "trailing in the vicinity of the Louvre and
howling [*heulend*] unto death." [10] His master, in all probability,
had been a foreigner who had traveled to Paris to defend freedom, and had been killed and buried anonymously in the course
of the uprising. Medor himself had been wounded along with his
master, but survived. Now what turned Medor into a (very un-
Baudelairean) hero of the populace is the fidelity with which he
stayed by his master's grave, long after his own recovery, for a
full seven months. "Several times already, he has been sold by
greedy owners to rich amateurs; he was taken some thirty hours'
distance from Paris; but he always rediscovered his way back." [11]
In his devotion, this creature of a foreigner in Paris (as Börne
was, as Benjamin soon would be) becomes the toast of the
people of Paris: their opera, their royal court, and their church. [12]

The transition from (lapsed) feral state to one of utter devotion to the memory of a human, the scheme informing Benjamin's script, structures what is perhaps the world's most famous dog story, Jack London's *Call of the Wild*. And it is the constellation formed by that work, or rather, by that work as read by Primo Levi, in conjunction with Benjamin's "True Dog Stories," that will open up the horizon onto which this reading will draw to a close. London's classic tale relates the traumatic seizure of the dog Buck from the estate in the "sun-kissed" Santa Clara Valley where he romped as "king," and his brutal "deportation," in a cagelike crate, to the Yukon, where he is harnessed into a team laboring for two prospectors during the gold rush of 1897. Under the "law of club and fang," in conditions of perpetual hunger, extreme cold, and general distrust of his fellow team members, Buck undergoes the "decay" of his "moral nature," as "instincts long dead" revive in him.[13] In brief, the "dominant primordial beast," a killer wolf, makes its return in Buck, amid conditions which, in human terms, seem akin to slave labor.[14]

In the second half of his novella, London's Buck, sold twice over, ends up being saved from death at the hands of an incompetent master by one John Thornton, for whom the dog experiences, for the first time, a "love that was feverish and burning, that was adoration, that was madness."[15] It is indeed Buck's love for Thornton that alone holds in check the feral strain that will eventually triumph in him after Thornton is killed in an Indian attack. Nonetheless, even after joining the wolf pack, Buck remains an anomaly. For every summer, he pays a visit to the burial spot of the only creature he ever loved. London's tale, in brief, which begins with the lapsing of a dog into feral behavior and ends with him nonetheless demonstrating an unfathomable and dog-like fidelity to the memory of a beloved human, has a structure quite similar to that informing Benjamin's radio script.

But it is precisely at this juncture that Primo Levi's essay on an Italian translation of *The Call of the Wild* reveals its pertinence.[16] For the author of the book translated into English as *Survival in Auschwitz* opens up what Benjamin calls a constellation by reading the London tale, almost in spite of himself, as though it were a prophecy of what he, a Jew, was to experience during World War II. Here, for instance, is Levi on the high point of the first part of the book, during which Buck's metamorphosis is initiated: Buck "feels being born within him 'the dominant primordial beast'; he subtly provokes the leader of the pack, encourages disorder, until he openly challenges Spitz (the 'lead dog'). This is the master page of the short book, and it is the fiercest: during a freezing night, surrounded by the starved but neutral pack, Spitz and Buck confront each other and Buck gets the better of him, thanks to his cleverness as a fighter: the loser is devoured on the spot by his former underlings. The next morning, Buck forces acceptance on his human masters: he has killed the leader of the team, he is the new team leader. He will be a chief (a *Kapo?*) even more efficient than Spitz, better at keeping order and discovering dangers along the track."[17] The parenthesis in the final sentence makes it clear that Levi could not but read London's tale of deportation to slave labor and perpetual hunger in a snowy clime as an allegory of what he would witness in Auschwitz. The particular vileness, moreover, corresponding to the outbreak of the feral strain in Buck, would lay in assuming the role of *Kapo,* pretending to enter into evil (or collaborate with it) in order to defeat it from within.

It was no doubt for that reason that Levi, unlike Benjamin, could have no truck with the implications of the second part of the London novella. For precisely where Benjamin tells his tale of Medor's superhuman fidelity to the memory of his deceased master, and London elaborates the relation that will have his Buck, as a member of the pack, nonetheless journeying every summer to mourn at the burial plot of Thornton, Levi balks: "Subjected to a deadly beating, he is saved by Thornton, the good prospector, and grows attached to him with total, exclusive love, the love of which only dogs are capable: and it's precisely here that, in my opinion, the book becomes weak. This devotion is excessive: where did the "dominant beast" go?"[18] And Levi concludes his piece by rejecting London's—and Benjamin's—own conclusion: "Buck has become the Ghost Dog, ferocious, nocturnal savager of prey and men; but every summer he goes in pilgrimage to the spot where Thornton is buried, the only creature whom the dog-turned-wolf ever loved. Come now: this is a bit too human." [19] The implication is that after the knowledge acquired in Auschwitz, as anticipated in the first part of the tale, a certain capacity for love would no longer be possible: something would have been extinguished, and its name, Levi all but confesses here, is love.

Benjamin and Levi are perhaps the two most haunting suicides of the twentieth century. The death of each persists in memory by virtue of its enigmatic—too early? too late?—relation to the genocide of the Jews. And it is "Wahre Geschichten von Hunden" that has allowed us, through the medium of Jack London's children's classic, to establish a communication between the two. In Benjamin's script, between the early evocation of the ferocity of those dogs apt to lapse into their feral state and the final tableau or *Trauerspiel* of Medor become the hero of popular sentiment, between nature and culture, then, there is an episode that strikes a curiously familiar note for anyone acquainted with the totality of the scripts for children. It concerns the cunning of a pack of dogs in Madagascar faced with the daunting task of traversing a river teeming with alligators eager to devour them. Their "trick" lay in assembling at one point along the river bank and howling until their would-be predators swam to their vicinity. Whereupon "the dogs immediately ran with all due haste up the bank and crossed a bit further on, without risk, since the alligators, in their clumsiness, were incapable of catching up with them." [20] The dogs of Madagascar, in brief, have thus already taken up the task of the "bootleggers" in the broadcast two months later: making one's way across the water without getting nabbed. In this, they join up with those practitioners of fraud that have been our concern since the beginning of these analyses in the paradigmatic case of the "Teezug." We have seen, moreover, how, from the archaic case of the robber bands in old

Germany (who knew a smattering of Hebrew) to that of Cagliostro (whom tradition had pegged as a Kabbalist), the series of scripts concerned with fraud bore a significant Judaic coefficient. So that the dogs cunningly making their way across the river in Madagascar link up with the series of tricksters that has been a principal component of the (crypto-Judaic) subtext we have observed at play in the entirety of the radio scripts.

Madagascar, moreover, bore its own Judaic context. For as of 1931, there would be numerous suggestions floated in France and Germany concerning a solution to the "Jewish question" in the form of a resettlement of European Jews in Madagascar.[21] Indeed, it was not until the infamous Wannsee Conference of January 1942 that Hitler himself relinquished the Madagascar "solution" in favor of genocide.[22] Thus, to return to our broader "canine" constellation, between Benjamin and Levi, the critic fleeing occupied Paris in 1940 and the devastated survivor of Auschwitz, but also between "nature" and "culture," on precisely that line of demarcation straddled by the "dog," and insistent as the locus of the "unconscious," we find Benjamin's pathetic pack, tricking its way to survival, on an island European diplomacy toyed with making the last hope of the Jews. The Madagascar "solution," and even more the experience of Levi, it will be objected, were in no way known to Benjamin at the time he set down "Wahre Geschichten von Hunden." But is not the unrecognized virtuality of his text, which would undergo such traumatic fulfillment in the course of time, not one measure of what might be construed as its "unconscious"? Unless, of course, advancing forward, one termed "unconscious" precisely what had been *repressed* in the blighted fulfillment of Benjamin's script: all that Levi could not take quite seriously in the "post-Auschwitz" half of London's *Call of the Wild;* more specifically, Buck's love for Thornton.

Beyond those valences of the term "unconscious," we would insist on the Madagascar crossing's phantasmal affinities with the problematic sketched in our reading of the children's radio scripts in their entirety. For if the river at the heart of "Wahre

Geschichten von Hunden," the line of demarcation between lupine ferocity and canine *Trauerspiel*, "nature" and "culture,"
may be superimposed on the "rum-line" being run by the bootleggers in the script of that name, it may also be superimposed
on the mobile line (in "Die Mississippi-Uberschwemmung
1927") formed by the Mississippi in its cataclysmic shifts east
and west. Whereby we rejoin the implicit subscript of *Aufklärung für Kinder*, the fusing of "fraud" and "catastrophe" in a
problematic we have termed Sabbatian.

To enter evil in order to defeat it from within . . . For Scholem, as we saw, such was the mystical mandate which became the
unacknowledged matrix of Jewish Enlightenment thought itself.
At an opposite extreme from *Aufklärung*, the will to defeat evil
from within finds what is perhaps its most hideous incarnation
in Primo Levi's evocation of Chaim Rumkowski. A more sinister
case than the Buck in whom Levi imagined a "Kapo,"
Rumkowski served as wartime president of the Lodz ghetto,
Nazi collaborator par excellence, and self-styled "King of the
Jews."[23] Levi: "Rumkowski was not only a renegade and an accomplice. In some measure, besides making people believe it, he
himself must have become progressively convinced that he was a
mashiach, a Messiah, a savior of his people, whose good he must,
at least intermittently, have desired. Paradoxically, his identification with the oppressor is flanked by, or perhaps alternates with
an identification with the oppressed. . . ."[24] Levi's Rumkowski,
then, is a "false Messiah," in the tradition of Scholem's Sabbatai
Zevi (or Jacob Frank), but eluding our judgment, in Levi's
words, "the way a compass needle goes wild at the magnetic
pole."[25] The work of Thomas Mann is adduced in evoking
Rumkowski's complexity.

In Scholem's life of Benjamin, there appears another falsely
messianic figure who, in fact, would end up as one of Thomas
Mann's characters. A man of "uncanny magnetic power," Oskar
Goldberg practiced a kind of aberrant "biological Kabbalah."[26]
What he aimed at was "the restoration of the magic bond be-
tween God and His people (of which he viewed himself as the

biological center). . . ."²⁷ In evoking Goldberg, Scholem speaks
of his "Luciferian luster" and, in his own memoirs, characterizes
him as "a representative of the devil in our generation."²⁸ Here
then was a man of uncommon authority among Jewish intellectuals in Berlin, whose disciples claimed he possessed "supernor-
mal abilities," and who was thought by Scholem to be Satanic:
a false messiah of genuinely Sabbatian stamp. And concerning Goldberg's group, Scholem tells us: "Benjamin's interest
in this Jewish sect [. . .] accompanied him right into the Hitler
period."²⁹

A charismatic and falsely messianic Jew in the Hitler period
. . . It is precisely at this quasi-mystical extreme from Enlightenment values that we encounter one of the central authors of the
Western liberal tradition, Primo Levi's choice for accommodating the contradictions of *his* "false messiah," Thomas Mann. In
Scholem's words: "the first novel of [Mann's] Joseph tetralogy,
The Tales of Jacob, is in its metaphysical sections based entirely
on Goldberg's book. This, to be sure, did not keep Mann from
making Goldberg the target of his irony a few years later in a
special chapter of his novel *Dr. Faustus.* There Goldberg appears
as the scholar Dr. Chaim Breisacher, a kind of metaphysical
super-Nazi who presents his magical racial theory largely in
Goldberg's own words."³⁰ Thus the fate of Goldberg was that
hinted at by Levi for Rumkowski, the Jewish fascist, waxing
falsely messianic in a novel by Thomas Mann. The Jew makes his
reentry into the most enlightened strain of German literature as
a caricatural representative of the paradoxical (or antinomian)
tradition we have seen at play between the scripts of *Aufklärung
für Kinder.*

There is a sense, of course, in which to have died before the
genocide is tantamount, in this last half of the twentieth century,
to having retained a certain innocence, even childhood. For
which reason we will conclude these pages on Benjamin's scripts
for children by examining a text that takes up elements that have
surfaced in our reading, but with a devastating hindsight—if not
maturity—that were denied to Benjamin himself. Near the

middle of a memoir of his own "maturity," *The Periodic Table,*
Primo Levi inserts a short story, written before the war, entitled
"Lead," and which was explicitly written, like so much of Benjamin, under the sign of Saturn.[31] It is the fantasy of one "Rodmund," an exiled native of Thiuda (Judah?), who is referred to
by his neighbors ("that is, our enemies") as "Alaman." In brief,
Rodmund would appear to be a German Jew. Now the narrator
belongs to a family which, from generation to generation, has
been faithful to its calling as miners of lead. If chemistry, the
author's profession, is in some sense construable in its historic
opposition to alchemy, Rodmund's trade is, in its way, no less an
exercise in anti-alchemy: he asks buyers to exchange gold for his
lead. Concerning that metal, he explains to a would-be pur-
chaser: "lead is actually the metal of death: because its weight is
a desire to fall, and to fall is a property of corpses, because its
very color is dulled-lead, because it is the metal of the planet
Tuisto, which is the slowest of planets, that is, the planet of the
dead."[32] Benjamin, in the enigmatically autobiographical text,
"Agesilaus Santander," had written: "I came into the world
under the sign of Saturn—the star of the slowest revolution, the
planet of detours and delays. . . ."[33] And as if to underscore the
link, Rodmund's interlocutor, in Levi's novel, responds: "that it
must be as I said, and that that planet is sacred to a god who in
his town was called Saturn."[34] The tale follows Rodmund, melancholic adept of Saturn, to an island "of metals." Perhaps the most
retrospectively sinister touch in the tale is the "plumes of
smoke" Rodmund observes from the foundries as he approaches
land.[35] He soon is drawn to a major deposit of lead—"turbid,
poisonous, and heavy"—and sets up his own slave-labor camp,
mining lead.[36]

The author, former inmate and slave laborer at Auschwitz,
makes mention of neither the sinister affinity between his prewar
fantasy ("Lead") and his own subsequent experience nor the reversal through which that affinity was consummated. The latter
part of the volume is in fact concerned not at all with fantasy, but
with Levi's twin activities as a chemist and a witness recording

his memories of Auschwitz, and the extent to which the two in some way may serve as metaphors of each other. In "Chromium," we are introduced to the author's professional specialty after the war, the chemistry of paints and varnishes: "It is an ancient art and therefore noble: its most remote testimony is in Genesis 6:14, where it is told how, in conformity with a precise specification of the Almighty, Noah coated (probably with a brush) the Ark's interior and exterior with melted pitch. But it is also a subtly fraudulent art, like that which aims at concealing the substratum by conferring on it the color and appearance of what it is not. . . ."[37] Thus do we encounter, at the heart of Levi's memoir, the twin motifs of fraudulence and catastrophe (the flood), whose meshing provided us with the subtext of Benjamin's radio scripts. As though the adult Levi, in the wake of his personal catastrophe, were seeking to piece his life together again on the basis of a structure that might have been absorbed on German radio during his childhood. The reference to Noah, moreover, places the motif of catastrophe explicitly in the context of redemption, whereby the "false messianism" of Benjamin's scripts seems pointedly at stake. As Levi, in those early years after the war, attempted to redeem his own past, he faced his first significant challenge as an industrial chemist, we read, in "redeeming" a shipment of damaged or "livered" paint. "Livering" refers to a tendency of paints, improperly prepared, to congeal or turn solid. Faced with the pile of (aptly named) "livers," Levi begins his inquiry into the preparation of the paint and discovers, after extensive detective work, that directions to add "2 or 3" drops of "a certain reagent" had been mistranscribed as "23" drops, thus resulting in a "flooding of the analysis."[38] Whereupon our Noah is set to redeem the batch, saving it from the "flood." The "therapy" selected is described as follows: "it was necessary to neutralize in some way, within the sick body of that varnish, the excess of basicity due to free lead oxide."[39] And indeed ammonium chloride turns out to work just that effect: "Angels and ministers of grace!—the paint was fluid and smooth, completely normal, born again from its ashes like the

Phoenix."[40] The redemption of the paint, thus paralleling a re-
claiming of his past (in the form of his writing "page after page
of the memories that were poisoning" him), has been effected by
a neutralization of (the effects of) lead oxide. But "Lead," we
have seen, was the title of the prewar fantasia that seemed to
place the author's surrogate, Rodmund, in the position of culprit, rather than victim, of a slave labor—or death—camp dis-
pensing the "poison" of lead. So that to neutralize lead oxide
would be tantamount to neutralizing (or repressing) a cor-
roded—or "oxidized"—version of that lingering fantasy. Such
would be the "subtly fraudulent labor" allowing Levi to redeem
the catastrophe. At which point the fusing of "fraudulence" and
"catastrophe," the stuff of Benjamin's radio scripts, the matrix of
what might be called his neo-Sabbatianism, would appear to
merge with repression itself. "Lead oxide," that is, the festering
fantasia of a certain undecidability, if only in fantasy, between
culprit and victim would join up with that other arch-chemical
of the Western unconscious, "trimethylamin," as it appears in
the specimen dream of *Die Traumdeutung*.[41]

What had been repressed returns, however, in a manner confirming our reading, toward the end of *The Periodic Table,* in a
chapter entitled "Vanadium." Levi here confronts his second major challenge as a chemist in the book: "no longer a "livered"
paint, but what is called in the jargon a "monkeyed" varnish, one
that hardens or dries prematurely. In seeking to redeem the small
catastrophe of a shipment of "monkeyed" varnish, Levi profits
from the suggestion of his German supplier, one Doktor L.
Müller, that the addition of .1 percent vanadium naphthenate
will solve the problem. But it is at this point that Levi's past in
Auschwitz intervenes. In observing that his informant has mis-
spelled the name of the radical "naphthenate" as "naptenate,"
our author suddenly recalls that this error was the characteristic
mistake of a Müller who had been his supervisor during his years
as an "educated slave" at the Buna rubber plant at Auschwitz.[42]
An inquiry confirms that the two Müllers are one and the same,
at which point an unsatisfactory correspondence between Levi

and his former slave-master begins, in the course of which our author fears above all his inability to deny Müller's humanity, to affirm any *essential* difference between them. Levi is distressed that Müller is able "hypocritically" to quote Levi's own words back to him, in a spirit of reconciliation.[43] But one can only wonder what response Levi would have come up with had Müller quoted back to him his own pre-war fantasy "Lead" . . .

Finally, Levi reluctantly agrees to meet, on the Italian Riviera, the man he feels he can no longer demonize or indeed view as essentially different from the normal gray run of humanity. He is saved from that feared interview by an announcement, a few days before it is to take place, that Müller had suddenly died "in his sixtieth year of life."[44] "Vanadium naphthenate," then, and all that it bore with it, revives the moral ambiguity which the "neutralization" of (the effects of) "lead oxide," the festering or corroding fantasy of "Lead," had succeeding in dispelling or repressing. In the economy of *The Periodic Table*, it effectively neutralized the neutralization of "lead oxide," effecting what may be called a return of the repressed. The result is a moral posture that would ultimately lead Levi, at the end of *Moments of Reprieve*, to claim that "we are all mirrored in Rumkowski, his ambiguity is ours. . . ."[45] The moral compass, to recall his image, goes wild.

The insistence on (the spelling of) the word or signifier "naphthenate," reminiscent of Freud's attachment to the dream letters of the formula for trimethylamin, takes on further resonance in this context. For early in the book, we are told that the author's "sustenance," during the prewar period, was Thomas Mann's novel *The Magic Mountain*.[46] Moreover, the portion of the novel that most fascinated him was "the political, theological, and metaphysical discussions between the humanist Settembrini and the Jewish Jesuit Naphta."[47] There is thus a chain of signifiers running through *The Periodic Table* from "Naphta" to "naphtenate" to "naphthenate." But Leo Naphta, the ex-Jewish nihilist and "reactionary revolutionist," whose taste for blood is traced by Mann back to his father's vocation as a ritual butcher, is, according to critical tradition, "the John the Baptist of fascism."[48] As such he is plainly an anticipation of Chaim Breisacher, the "Jewish fascist" of *Dr. Faustus,* said to be modeled on Oskar Goldberg, the bogus messiah of Scholem's memoir of Benjamin. Again: the Jew as proto-Nazi. It is thus ultimately through Mann's two novels that a communication between Benjamin and Levi may be established.[49]

But if Breisacher was in some sense originally Naphta, he can be said to be derived only secondarily from Oskar Goldberg. And if the "Jewish Jesuit" Naphta is already the Jew Breisacher, Naphta in some crucial way would appear, beyond his conversion, to remain Jewish. With Breisacher emerging out of Scholem's memoir of Benjamin, and Naphta a reminiscence of Levi's memoir of his own life, we are thus confronted, at the heart of two masterworks of the European novel, legacies of the *Bildungsideal* of the Western Enlightenment, with two images of the self-divided or antinomian Jew, having entered, for whatever reason, so deeply into evil that one is hard put to imagine him finding his way out. Breisacher and Naphta would thus constitute phantasmal signatures of a sort, less of their author than of their ideal (albeit virtual) Jewish readers: the "Satanic" Benjamin of "Agesilaus Santander," the Levi of *The Periodic Table* whose moral compass was sent in a spin after recognizing a misspelling of "naphthenate." As such the two Mann characters are reminiscences of that aberrantly messianic will to defeat evil from within whose subterranean presence has been traced by Scholem to the Sabbatian movement. Evil, of course, has undergone its own evolution, assuming forms at once more spectacular and more banal. But the continuity is clear: the European "Jewish fascist" is but the century's limit case for imagining a Jew's disastrous and willful entry into evil.[50]

Beyond the dreams of Benjamin and Levi, Mann's novels appear to offer their own commentary on the Enlightenment dream of assimilation and its relation to evil. For when these works do succeed in assimilating Jews, it is in the form of the bewitched paragons of "revolutionary conservatism," Naphta and Breisacher.[51] As though, following Scholem, the transgressive core of Sabbatianism were still alive at the heart of Enlightenment itself. It is a configuration which survives in what has recently been called the two Holocausts: the linguistic and imaginative contamination operative between the consecrated term for the Jewish genocide, evil itself, and that "silent Holocaust" of Jewish self-denial which is the daily mode of ordinary Jewish life in the West.[52] Less the banality of evil, then, than a certain evil insistent in banality itself. That such a perspective should already be implicit in Benjamin's radio scripts for children, only to reach fruition, on the other side of catastrophe, in Levi's record of his own achievement of "maturity," is one of the more surprising upshots of our reading. The concatenation of terms binding the Levi memoir to the Benjamin scripts—the sign of Saturn; catastrophe and fraud; the characters from Mann—stands in confirmation. That these two exemplary Jewish writers of the century should also be its most exemplary suicides is a factor whose pertinence to these reflections seems open to more than mere speculation.

NOTES

1. CHILDHOOD

1. The two programs were the "Jugendstunde" of the Berlin Funkstunde and the "Stunde der Jugend" of the Sudwestdeutschen Rundfunk of Frankfurt. For a listing of the dates of Benjamin's participation in these and other radio programs, as well as a discussion of his activities in, and thought on, the new medium, see Sabine Schiller-Lerg's informative *Walter Benjamin und der Rundfunk: Programmarbeit zwischen Theorie und Praxis* (Munich: K. G. Saur, 1984). In the wake of her important study of the Arcades Project, *The Dialectics of Seeing: Walter Benjamin and the Arcades Project* (Cambridge: MIT Press, 1989), Susan Buck-Morss has commented provocatively on the radio scripts for children in "'Verehrte Unsichtbare!': Walter Benjamins Radiovorträge," in *Walter Benjamin und die Kinderliteratur: Aspekte der Kinderkultur in den zwanziger Jahren,* ed. Klaus Doderer (Weinheim: Juventa Verlag, 1988), pp. 93–101.

2. For the history of the radio manuscripts, see Rolf Tiedemann's editor's note to Walter Benjamin, *Aufklärung für Kinder* (Frankfurt: Suhrkamp, 1985), pp. 206–8.

3. When the radio scripts were incorporated into volume 7 of the *Gesammelte Schriften* ed. Rolf Tiedemann and Hermann Schweppenhäuser in collaboration with Christoph Gödde, Henri Lonitz, and Gary Smith (Frankfurt: Suhrkamp, 1989), pp. 69–249, the title *Aufklärung fur Kinder* was replaced by the more neutral "Rundfunkgeschichten für Kinder." For a discussion of Benjamin's own reservations about Enlightenment, see Anson Rabinbach, "Between Enlightenment and Apocalypse: Benjamin, Bloch and Modern German Jewish Messianism," in *New German Critique* 34 (Winter 1985), pp. 78–124. In his 1918 essay "Program of the Coming Philosophy," translated by Mark Ritter in *The Philosophical Forum* 15 (Fall-Winter 1983–84), p. 42, Benjamin, characterizing Kant's "experience" as "the same as that of the Enlightenment," goes on to say that it "was an experience or a view of the lowest order."

4. The most provocative reading of what was at stake in Benjamin's vexed relations with the university system is Irving Wohlfarth's "Resentment Begins at Home: Nietzsche, Benjamin, and the University," in *On Walter Benjamin: Critical Essays and Recollections,* ed. Gary Smith (Cambridge, MIT Press, 1988), pp. 224–59.

5. Gershom Scholem, *Walter Benjamin: The Story of a Friendship,* trans. Harry Zohn (New York: Schocken, 1981), p. 129.

6. Ibid., p. 148.

7. Paul de Man, in *The Resistance to Theory* (Minneapolis: University of Minnesota Press, 1986), offers a reading of "The Task of the Translator" that is deconstructive in its anti-messianism. For a critique of that reading, see my "Prosopopeia Revisited," in *Romanic Review,* 81, 1 (January 1990), pp. 137–43. For a different articulation of the concerns of deconstruction with Benjamin's thought, see the conclusion of my *Legacies: Of Anti-Semitism in France* (Minneapolis: University of Minnesota Press, 1983), pp. 83–90. In *The Dialectics of Seeing,* p. 338, Susan Buck-Morss offers a brief critique of deconstruction from a Benjaminian perspective.

8. It was not until years after I wrote *Revolution and Repetition: Marx/Hugo/Balzac* (Berkeley: University of California Press, 1977), with its insistence on the freezing of dialectic in *The Eighteenth Brumaire of Louis Bonaparte,* that the publication of *Das Passagen-Werk,* ed. Rolf Tiedemann (Frankfurt: Suhrkamp, 1982), revealed to me just how unwittingly close to Benjamin's notion of a "dialectic at a standstill" I had been treading. I have since discussed the mediating potential (between Marx and Benjamin) of the writings of Georges Sorel, with their alternately positive and negative valuations of stalled dialectics, in "Georges Sorel's Dreyfusard Revolution," in *Proceedings of the Hofstra University Bicentennial for the French Revolution* (forthcoming). For a critique of my reading of Marx in a Benjaminian context, see Terry Eagleton, *Walter Benjamin or Towards a Revolutionary Criticism* (London: Verso, 1981), pp. 162–69.

9. *Das Passagen-Werk,* vol. 2, p. 1053. (All translations from *Das Passagen-Werk* and *Aufklärung für Kinder* are mine.)

10. Ibid., vol. 1, p. 98.

11. Ibid., vol. 2, p. 1058.

12. Ibid., vol. 2, p. 1053.

13. Letter of 25 January 1930 in Walter Benjamin, *Briefe,* ed. Gershom Scholem and Theodor W. Adorno (Frankfurt: Suhrkamp, 1978), vol. 2, p. 509.

14. "Berliner Spielzeugwanderung II," in *Aufklärung für Kinder,* p. 49.

15. Walter Benjamin, "Spielzeug und Spielen," in *Uber Kinder, Jugend und Erziehung* (Frankfurt: Suhrkamp, 1969), p. 67.

16. Ibid., p. 67.

17. Ibid., p. 68.

18. See Jean Laplanche, *Nouveaux fondements pour la psychanalyse: La Séduction originaire* (Paris: P.U.F., 1987). For a discussion of the implications of Laplanche's reading of Freud for the understanding of literature, see my "Mallarmé and 'Seduction Theory'," in *Paragraph*, vol. 14, 1991. The perspective in that essay is ultimately compatible with the view of Mallarmé found, in passing, in Benjamin's "Berlin Chronicle," in *Reflections*, ed. Peter Demetz, trans. Edmund Jephcott (New York: Harcourt Brace Jovanovich, 1978), p. 35: "These words that exist on the frontier between two linguistic regions, of children and of adults, are comparable to those of Mallarmé's poems, which the conflict between the poetic and the profane word has as it were consumed and made evanescent, airy." Laplanche himself has attempted a reading of "The Task of the Translator" in "Le mur et l'arcade," in *Nouvelle revue de psychanalyse*, 37 (Spring 1988), pp. 95–110.

19. "Spielzeug und Spielen," p. 71.

20. For a discussion of the mimetic or identificatory bases of narcissism in Freud, see Jean Laplanche, *Life and Death in Psychoanalysis*, trans. Jeffrey Mehlman (Baltimore: Johns Hopkins University Press, 1976), pp. 66–84.

21. "Spielzeug und Spielen," p. 72.

22. Scholem, *Walter Benjamin*, p. 22.

23. See ibid., p. 143.

24. Walter Benjamin, "Aussicht ins Kinderbuch," in *Uber Kinder, Jugend und Erziehung*, p. 47.

25. Ibid., p. 49.

26. Sigmund Freud, *The Interpretation of Dreams*, trans. James Strachey (New York: Avon, 1965), p. 545. I have discussed the significance of that footnote in "Trimethylamin: Notes on Freud's Specimen Dream," in *Diacritics*, 6, 1 (1976), pp. 42–45.

27. For a recent (and representative) self-portrait of a "recovering Francophile," see Nancy Miller, *Getting Personal: Autobiographical Acts and Other Feminist Favors* (New York: Routledge, 1991).

28. *Briefe*, vol. 2, p. 779.

29. See Harry Zohn's English translation, in *Charles Baudelaire: A Lyric Poet in the Era of High Capitalism* (London: New Left Books, 1973).

30. "Die Bootleggers," read over Berlin radio on 8 November 1930 and printed in *Aufklärung für Kinder*, p. 151.

31. Freud, *Jokes and Their Relation to the Unconscious*, trans. James Strachey (New York: Norton, 1963), p. 115.

32. Ibid., p. 247.

33. "Rastelli erzählt . . .," in *Gesammelte Schriften,* ed. Rolf Tiedemann and Hermann Schweppenhäuser (Frankfurt: Suhrkamp, 1972), vol. 4, p. 778.

34. Ibid., p. 780.

35. "Franz Kafka: On the Tenth Anniversary of His Death," in Benjamin, *Illuminations,* ed. Hannah Arendt, trans. Harry Zohn (New York: Schocken, 1969), p. 112.

36. Ibid.

37. Charles Baudelaire, "Une mort héroïque," in *Le Spleen de Paris,* in *Oeuvres complètes,* ed. Y.-G. Le Dantec and Claude Pichois (Paris: Gallimard, 1961), p. 272. For a discussion of the prose poem in terms of its interruption of dialectic, see my "Baudelaire with Freud: Theory and Pain," in *Diacritics,* 4, 1 (Spring 1974), pp. 7–13.

38. "Une mort héroïque," p. 272.

39. "Rastelli erzählt . . . ," p. 780.

40. Scholem, *Walter Benjamin,* p. 135.

41. Performed over Berlin radio on 4 February 1932, and over Frankfurt radio on 30 March 1932.

42. *Das Passagen-Werk,* p. 1062.

43. "Die Eisenbahnkatastrophe vom Firth of Tay," in *Aufklärung für Kinder,* p. 178.

44. *Das Passagen-Werk,* p. 46.

45. *Aufklärung für Kinder,* p. 179.

46. Ibid., p. 180.

47. Ibid.

48. Benjamin, "Eduard Fuchs, Collector and Historian," in *One-Way Street and Other Writings,* trans, Edmund Jephcott and Kingsley Shorter (London: New Left Books, 1979), p. 358.

49. *Aufklärung für Kinder,* p. 181.

50. Ibid., p. 182.

51. *Das Passagen-Werk,* p. 46.

52. *Aufklärung für Kinder,* p. 183.

53. "The Task of the Translator," in *Illuminations,* p. 79.

54. Hannah Arendt, "Introduction: Walter Benjamin, 1892–1940" in *Illuminations,* p. 49.

55. "Karl Kraus," in *Reflections,* p. 266.

56. Ibid., p. 268.

57. The date of broadcast of this script has not been established. See Schiller-Lerg, *Walter Benjamin und der Rundfunk,* p. 533.

58. "Briefmarkenschwindel," in *Aufklärung für Kinder,* p. 141.

59. Ibid.

60. Ibid., p. 142.

61. Ibid.
62. Ibid.
63. Ibid., p. 145.
64. Ibid.
65. Jacques Derrida, *Mémoires: For Paul de Man* (New York: Columbia University Press, 1986).
66. For a cogent discussion of Benjamin's essay, see Richard Wolin, *Walter Benjamin: An Aesthetic of Redemption* (New York: Columbia University Press), p. 191.
67. "The Work of Art in the Age of Mechanical Reproduction," in *Illuminations,* p. 220.
68. *Aufklärung für Kinder,* p. 140.
69. Ibid., p. 195.
70. *Das Passagen-Werk,* p. 53.
71. Ibid., p. 56.
72. Ibid.
73. *Illuminations,* p. 226.
74. Ibid.
75. Ibid.
76. Ibid., p. 224.
77. Baudelaire, *Oeuvres complètes,* p. 306.
78. See my "Baudelaire with Freud: Theory and Pain," in *Diacritics,* 4, 1 (Spring 1974), pp. 7–13.
79. *Briefe,* p. 795.
80. The two poems are nicely juxtaposed on pages 24 and 27 of Daniel Leuwers's recent anthology, *Poètes français des XIXme et XXme siècles* (Paris: Livre de poche, 1987).
81. Baudelaire, *Oeuvres complètes,* p. 299.
82. Ibid., p. 300.
83. "Berliner Kindheit um Neunzehnhundert," in *Gesammelte Schriften,* vol. 4, p. 251.
84. Ibid.
85. Ibid., p. 252.
86. *Aufklärung für Kinder,* p. 33.
87. Broadcast in Berlin on 18 September 1931.
88. *Das Passagen-Werk,* p. 99.
89. Ibid., p. 155.
90. Ibid.
91. Proust too was taken with the prose of Léon Daudet, whose role in his career as well as in those of Bernanos and Céline make of him arguably the most important French literary critic of the twentieth century. For a discussion of Proust's moral dilemma in subscribing, for aesthetic reasons,

to *Action Française,* see my "Literature and Collaboration: Benoist-Méchin's Return to Proust," in *Lacan and Narration: The Psychoanalytic Difference in Narrative Theory,* ed. Robert Con Davis (Baltimore: Johns Hopkins University Press, 1983), pp. 968–82.

92. "A Berlin Chronicle," in *Reflections,* p. 5.

93. "Berliner Chronik," in *Gesammelte Schriften,* vol. 6, p. 469. (The English translation, "A Berlin Chronicle," omits this passage.) *Aufklärung für Kinder,* p. 160.

94. *Aufklärung für Kinder,* p. 162.

95. Ibid., p. 163.

96. Ibid., p. 182. At this juncture, we may already intuit the link between the radio scripts and Benjamin at his most "messianic." In his jottings for the "Theses on the Philosophy of History," we read (*Gesammelte Schriften,* vol. 1, p. 1233): "The dialectical image is a flash of ball lightning (*ein Kugelblitz*) that traverses the whole horizon of the past." The passage is discussed in Irving Wohlfarth, "On the Messianic Structure of Walter Benjamin's Last Reflections," in *Glyph* 3 (Baltimore: Johns Hopkins University Press, 1978), p. 186.

97. *Aufklärung für Kinder,* pp. 163–64.

98. Ibid., p. 163.

99. Ibid., p. 142.

100. "Oblitération" is, in fact, the term used by Sylvie Muller in her recent translation of the radio scripts. See Benjamin, *Lumières pour enfants: Emissions pour la jeunesse* (Paris: Christian Bourgois, 1988), p. 191.

101. *Aufklärung für Kinder,* p. 161.

102. Ibid., p. 165.

103. The translation is John Ciardi's, in Dante, *The Inferno* (New York: New American Library, 1954), p. 135.

104. George Santayana, *Three Philosophical Poets* (New York: Doubleday, 1938), p. 104.

105. "Eduard Fuchs, Collector and Historian," p. 105.

106. "One-Way Street," in *One-Way Street and Other Writings,* p. 92.

107. "Erdbeben von Lissabon" was broadcast over Berlin radio on 31 October 1931.

108. *Aufklärung für Kinder,* p. 166.

109. *Gesammelte Schriften,* vol. 4, pp. 761–63.

110. Voltaire, *Correspondance,* ed. Theodore Besterman (Geneva: Institut et Musée Voltaire, 1953–65), vol. 28, p. 157.

111. The passage is related to Voltaire's *Candide* in George Havens's Introduction to his edition of that work (New York: Holt Rinehart and Winston, 1969), p. xxxvi.

112. *Aufklärung für Kinder,* p. 169.

113. Ibid., p. 167.

114. Ibid., p. 169.

115. "Die Mississippi-Uberschwemmung 1927" was broadcast over Berlin radio on 23 March 1932. A week later, the Berlin script on the Firth of Tay was rebroadcast in Frankfurt. Benjamin's final script for children's radio, "Von Seeräubern und Piraten," broadcast in Berlin on 19 January 1933, has been lost.

116. *Aufklärung für Kinder,* p. 184.

117. Ibid.

118. Ibid.

119. Ibid.

120. Ibid.

121. "The Task of the Translator," in *Illuminations,* p. 71.

122. Ibid., p. 78.

123. Ibid., p. 81.

124. Ibid., p. 82.

125. *Aufklärung für Kinder,* p. 125.

126. Ibid., p. 186.

127. Ibid.

128. See Laplanche's important analysis of the passage in *Life and Death in Psychoanalysis,* p. 62.

129. *Aufklärung für Kinder,* p. 187.

130. Ibid., p. 188.

131. Scholem, *Walter Benjamin,* p. 179.

132. Cited in Wolin, *Walter Benjamin: An Aesthetic of Redemption,* p. ix.

133. See Lisa Fittko, "The Story of Old Benjamin," in *Das Passagen-Werk,* p. 1186.

134. *Aufklärung für Kinder,* p. 187.

135. Ibid., p. 188.

136. Fittko, "The Story of Old Benjamin," in *Das Passagen-Werk,* p. 1193. Hermann Grab's letter from Lisbon of 10 October 1940 to Adorno, however, suggests that given the considerable time it took Benjamin to expire, his supply of morphine could not have been very great. See letter reproduced in Hans Puttnies and Gary Smith, *Benjaminiana* (Giessen: Anabas, 1991), pp. 217–19.

137. Letter of Grete Freund, Lisbon, 10 October 1940, in *Das Passagen-Werk,* p. 1195.

138. *Aufklärung für Kinder,* p. 148.

139. Ibid., p. 151.

140. *Illuminations*, p. 78. For a discussion of the "breaking of the vessels" in Lurianic Kabbalah, see Gershom Scholem, *Major Trends in Jewish Mysticism* (New York: Schocken, 1941), p. 266.

141. *Illuminations*, p. 78.

142. "Neapel" was broadcast in Frankfurt on 9 May 1931.

143. For a discussion of the broader significance of "Naples" for Benjamin, see Susan Buck-Morss, *The Dialectics of Seeing*, p. 27.

144. Schiller-Lerg, *Walter Benjamin und der Rundfunk*, p. 100.

145. Benjamin, *Reflections*, p. 165.

146. Benjamin, *Gesammelte Schriften*, vol. 4, p. 309.

147. See letter of 10 May 1924 to Scholem, in *Briefe*, vol. 1, p. 344.

148. The point is made implicitly by Susan Buck-Morss in *The Dialectics of Seeing*, p. 9.

149. Benjamin, *Illuminations*, p. 253.

150. Benjamin, *Kinder, Jugend und Erziehung*, p. 83.

151. Benjamin's (tendentially Marxist) links with Brecht may also be detected in "Theaterbrand in Canton," a script about a disastrous nineteenth-century fire in a Chinese theater. For Brecht's debt to Chinese dramaturgy had been commented on in "What is Epic Theater?" (*Illuminations*, p. 148). The script is striking in its insistence on the Benjaminian motif of awakening from a dream as a quintessential theatrical subject. The play—or dream—from which the catastrophic fire awakens its audience is centered on the sacrificial flame of the temple of a war god. Might the apocalypse be readable as an awakening from fascism?

152. *Das Passagen-Werk*, p. 1050.

153. *Illuminations*, p. 257.

154. Ibid., p. 263, 261.

155. Ibid., p. 106.

156. It was a preoccupation that would issue many years later in Scholem's, *Sabbatai Sevi: The Mystical Messiah*, trans. R. J. Z. Werblowsky (Princeton: Princeton University Press, 1973).

157. Scholem, *Walter Benjamin*, p. 136.

158. Ibid., p. 136.

159. Ibid.

160. *Major Trends in Jewish Mysticism*, pp. 287–324.

161. Ibid., p. 308.

162. Ibid., p. 288.

163. *Das Passagen-Werk*, p. 574.

164. *Illuminations*, p. 261.

165. Georges Sorel, *Les Illusions du progrès* (Paris: Rivière, 1908). The work is listed as Item 726 in Benjamin's register of books he had read (*Gesammelte Schriften*, 7, p. 447).

166. *Major Trends in Jewish Mysticism,* p. 300.

167. *Das Passagen-Werk,* p. 75.

168. Ibid.

169. Ibid., p. 76.

170. Auguste Blanqui, *L'Eternité par les astres* (Paris: Editions de la Tête de Feuilles, 1972), p. 139.

171. Ibid.

172. Ibid., p. 140.

173. *Illuminations,* p. 260.

174. *Major Trends in Jewish Mysticism,* p. 305.

175. Ibid.

176. Gershom Scholem, "Redemption Through Sin," in *The Messianic Idea in Judaism* (New York: Schocken, 1971), p. 126.

177. Ibid., p. 109.

178. Walter Benjamin, *The Origin of German Tragic Drama,* trans. John Osborne (London: NLB, 1977), p. 183.

179. Ibid., p. 174.

180. *The Messianic Idea in Judaism,* p. 109.

181. *The Origin of German Tragic Drama,* p. 175.

182. *Major Trends in Jewish Mysticism,* p. 311.

183. *The Origins of German Tragic Drama,* p. 176.

184. *Illuminations,* p. 254.

185. *Major Trends in Jewish Mysticism,* p. 308.

186. The script for "Dr. Faust" was broadcast over Berlin radio on 30 January 1931.

187. *Aufklärung für Kinder,* p. 126.

188. Ibid., p. 131.

189. Ibid., p. 126.

190. "Hexenprozesse" was broadcast over Berlin radio on 16 July 1930.

191. *Aufklärung für Kinder,* p. 90.

192. Ibid.

193. Ibid., p. 92.

194. Ibid.

195. This script was broadcast in Frankfurt on 23 September 1930, then in Berlin on 2 October 1930.

196. *Aufklärung für Kinder,* p. 101.

197. Ibid., p. 97.

198. Ibid., p. 99. Scholem, in *Walter Benjamin,* p. 85, recalls an episode of 1919: "As a gift I had sent [Benjamin] the new edition of Avé-Lallemant's *Das deutsche Gaunertum* [Criminals of Germany], a book which contained an extensive discussion of the Jewish underworld in its relationship to the German one—a subject considered taboo by Jewish historiography but one

that began to attract me greatly as complementary to the Jewish 'upper-world' of mysticism. 'The crooks as God's people—that would be a move-ment'—so I wrote at the time." The subject of Jewish elements among Ger-man thieves was thus rife with Kabbalistic overtones.

199. "Cagliostro" was broadcast in Frankfurt on 14 February 1931.

200. *Aufklärung für Kinder,* p. 133.

201. Ibid.

202. Thomas Carlyle, "Count Cagliostro," in *Critical and Miscellaneous Essays* (New York: Scribner's, 1899), p. 266; and Gérard de Nerval, "Du mysticisme révolutionnaire," in *Oeuvres* (Paris: Flammarion, 1966).

203. "Le mysticisme révolutionnaire," p. 322.

204. Carlyle, "Count Cagliostro," p. 293.

205. Ibid., p. 303.

206. Ibid., p. 286.

207. *Aufklärung für Kinder,* p. 136.

208. Carlyle, "Count Cagliostro," p. 263.

209. Ibid., p. 289.

210. Ibid., p. 278.

211. *Major Trends in Jewish Mysticism,* p. 317.

212. *Aufklärung für Kinder,* pp. 137–38.

213. Carlyle, "Count Cagliostro," p. 268.

214. Ibid., p. 269.

215. *Major Trends in Jewish Mysticism,* p. 315.

216. Ibid., p. 309.

217. *The Messianic Idea in Judaism,* p. 84.

218. "Du mysticisme révolutionnaire," p. 323, 332.

219. *The Messianic Idea in Judaism,* p. 126.

220. Ibid., p. 137.

221. *Du Frankisme au jacobinisme* (Paris: Gallimard, Le Seuil, 1982).

222. *Major Trends in Jewish Mysticism,* p. 308.

223. Carlyle, "Count Cagliostro," p. 293.

224. *Aufklärung für Kinder,* p. 136.

225. Carlyle, "Count Cagliostro," p. 286.

226. On the notion of *apokatastasis* in Benjamin's messianism, see Irv-ing Wohlfarth, "Et Cetera?: De l'historien comme chiffonnier," in *Walter Benjamin à Paris,* ed. Heinz Wismann (Paris: Editions du Cerf, 1986), pp. 596–609.

227. In this sense, the "Cagliostro" script would approximate the con-dition which Benjamin, after Goethe, thought of as that of an *Urphänomen:* specimen of a corpus whose theory it seems already to be.

228. Carlyle, "Count Cagliostro," p. 273.

229. *Aufklärung für Kinder,* p. 102.

230. Ibid., p. 108. "Die Zigeuner" was broadcast in Berlin on 23 October 1930.

231. Ibid., p. 137.

232. "Berliner Dialekt" was broadcast on 9 November 1929; "Borsig" on 5 April 1930; "Besuch im Messingwerk" on 24 May 1930; the script for "Fontanes 'Wanderungen durch die Mark Brandenburg'" is undated.

233. "Das dämonische Berlin" was broadcast on 25 February 1930.

234. *Aufklärung für Kinder,* p. 27.

235. Ibid., p. 29.

236. Ibid.

237. *Gesammelte Schriften,* vol. 4, p. 285.

238. Ibid., p. 284.

239. "Ein Berliner Strassenjunge" was broadcast on 7 March 1930; "Die Mietskaserne" on 12 April 1930.

240. *Aufklärung für Kinder,* p. 33.

241. Ibid., p. 35.

242. *Reflections,* p. 7.

243. *Aufklärung für Kinder,* p. 37.

244. *Gesammelte Schriften,* vol. 6, p. 469. The passage is not included in the English translation of "A Berlin Chronicle" in *Reflections.*

245. Ibid., p. 491.

246. *Aufklärung für Kinder,* p. 59.

247. Ibid., p. 60.

248. Ibid.

249. Ibid., p. 64.

250. Georges Bataille, "Le labyrinthe," in *Oeuvres complètes* (Paris: Gallimard, 1970), vol. 1, pp. 433–41.

251. Georges Bataille, *L'expérience intérieure* (Paris: Gallimard, 1954), p. 112.

252. Denis Hollier, *La Prise de la Concorde: Essais sur Georges Bataille* (Paris: Gallimard, 1974), p. 133.

253. Pierre Klossowski has evoked Benjamin's presence at the Collège de sociologie, cofounded by Bataille, during his last years in Paris, in "Between Marx and Fourier," trans. Susan Z. Bernstein, in Gary Smith, ed., *On Walter Benjamin: Critical Essays and Recollections,* pp. 367–70.

254. *Das Passagen-Werk,* p. 57.

255. *Aufklärung für Kinder,* p. 62.

256. *The Messianic Idea in Judaism,* p. 99.

257. Georges Bataille, *L'Erotisme* (Paris: Minuit, 1957), p. 70.

258. "Berliner Spielzeugwanderung" was broadcast on 15 and 22 March 1930.

259. *Aufklärung für Kinder,* p. 40.

260. Ibid., p. 41.
261. Ibid., p. 42.
262. *Das Passagen-Werk,* p. 50.
263. Ibid., p. 1055.
264. Ibid., p. 51.
265. Scholem, *Walter Benjamin,* p. 135.
266. *Gesammelte Schriften,* vol. 4, p. 251.
267. Ibid., p. 252.
268. Ibid., p. 247.
269. An additional and striking realization of the same structure is found in the proto-"expressionist" sonnet entitled "Wahlverwandtschaften [Elective Affiniites]," which Zacharias Werner sent to Goethe, and which Benjamin, whatever his misgivings about Werner's interpretation of Goethe's novel, included in its entirety in the body of his 1922 essay on *Die Wahlverwandtschaften (Gesammelte Schriften,* vol. 1, p. 142):

> Vorbei an Gräbern und an Leichensteinen
> Die schön vermummt die sichre Beut'erwarten
> Hin schlängelt sich der Weg nach Edens Garten
> Wo Jordan sich und Acheron vereinen.
>
> Erbaut auf Triebsand will getürmt erscheinen
> Jerusalem; allein die grässlich zarten
> Meernixe, die sechstausend Jahr schon harrten,
> Lechzen im See, durch Opfer sich zu reinen.
>
> Da kommt ein heilig freches Kind gegangen
> Des Heiles Engel trägts, den Sohn der Sünden,
> Der See schlingt alles! Weh uns!—Es war Scherz!
>
> Will Helios die Erde denn entzünden?
> Er glüht ja nur sie liebend zu umfangen!
> Du darfst den Halbgott lieben, zitternd Herz!

The poem, in retrospect, reads as an astonishing allegory of what would be the course of Benjamin's life: the appearance of a will toward Zion, the pagan drowning of that aspiration, the suggestion of a holocaust (Helios was Werner's name for Goethe) only half-dispelled by the notion that the burning is with love. That "love," then, would correspond to the "sexual awakening" of *Berliner Kindheit* even as the will to Jerusalem would find its counterpart in the failed visit to the synagogue in the later text.
270. "Agesilaus Santander," in Scholem, "Walter Benjamin and His Angel," in *On Jews and Judaism in Crisis* (New York: Schocken, 1976), p. 206. Scholem's interpretation of the text has been challenged by Werner Fuld, in *Walter Benjamin: Zwischen den Stühlen* (Frankfurt: S. Fischer, 1981).
271. "Agesilaus Santander," ibid., p. 207.
272. Ibid., p. 213.

273. *Charles Baudelaire: Un poète lyrique à l'apogée du capitalisme,* trans. Jean Lacoste (Paris: Payot, 1982), p. 27.

274. For a discussion of Gide's reaction to Céline's work, see my *Legacies: Of Anti-Semitism in France,* p. 88.

275. Scholem, *Walter Benjamin,* pp. 212, 213.

276. *Reflections,* p. 5.

277. Léon Daudet, *Paris vécu* (Paris: Gallimard, 1969), p. 243.

278. Louis Aragon, *Le paysan de Paris* (Paris: Gallimard, 1926), p. 35.

279. Benjamin, *Briefe,* vol. 2, p. 663.

280. Georges Bernanos, *La grande peur des bien-pensants* (Paris: Grasset, 1931), p. 318.

281. Scholem, *Walter Benjamin,* p. 217.

282. *Reflections,* p. 261. For a discussion of Léon Bloy and his relation to French anti-Semitism, see my *Legacies: Of Anti-Semitism in France,* pp. 23–33.

283. *Reflections,* p. 272.

284. Scholem, "Walter Benjamin and His Angel," p. 207.

285. *Reflections,* p. 251.

286. See my "How to Read Freud on Jokes: The Critic as *Schadchen,*" in *New Literary History,* 6, 2 (Winter 1975), pp. 439–61.

287. See Irving Wohlfarth, "Et Cetera?: De l'historien comme chiffonnier," p. 564.

288. Benjamin, *Briefe,* vol. 2, p. 787.

289. Ibid., vol. 1, p. 446.

290. Aragon, *Le paysan de Paris,* p. 36.

291. For a discussion of Giraudoux's anti-Semitism and its relation to his literary career, see my *Legacies: Of Anti-Semitism in France,* pp. 34–63.

292. Jean Giraudoux, *La Folle de Chaillot* in *Théâtre* (Paris: Grasset, 1959), p. 177.

293. Ibid., p. 124.

294. Scholem, *Walter Benjamin,* p. 204. For elaboration of the analysis of Giraudoux in this paragraph, see my *Legacies: Of Anti-Semitism in France,* chapter 3.

295. Jean Giraudoux, "Divertissement de Siegfried," in *N.R.F.* (July 1928).

296. Hannah Arendt, *The Origins of Totalitarianism* (New York: Harcourt Brace Jovanovich, 1951), pp. 106–17.

2. MATURITY

1. Despite its placement in the anthology, "Wahre Geschichten von Hunden" was in fact broadcast (from Berlin) relatively early in Benjamin's radio career, on 17 September 1930.

2. *Aufklärung für Kinder,* p. 128.

3. Ibid., p. 191.

4. The classic philosophical development of the theme is in "Independence and Dependence of Self-Consciousness: Lordship and Bondage," section B, chapter IV, subchapter A, of Hegel, *The Phenomenology of Mind,* trans. J. B. Baillie (New York: Harper, 1967), pp. 228–40. In George Lichtheim's "editor's summary" (p. 228): "Servitude is not only a phase of human history, it is in principle a condition of the development and maintenance of the consciousness of self as a fact of experience."

5. We inflect to our own use here one of the more important of Benjamin's concepts. For a discussion of the "method of 'Dialectic at a Standstill' and its relation to the theory of "dialectical images" in Benjamin, see Richard Wolin, *Walter Benjamin: An Aesthetic of Redemption,* p. 125.

6. *Aufklärung für Kinder,* p. 192.

7. Jean Laplanche, *Life and Death in Psychoanalysis,* chapter 5, "Aggressiveness and Sadomasochism."

8. *Aufklärung für Kinder,* p. 194.

9. Ibid.

10. Ibid., p. 195.

11. Ibid.

12. Ibid.

13. Jack London, *The Call of the Wild* (New York: New American Library, 1960), pp. 28, 29.

14. Ibid., p. 42.

15. Ibid., p. 63.

16. Primo Levi, "Jack London's Buck," in *The Mirror Maker,* trans. Raymond Rosenthal (New York: Schocken, 1989), pp. 149–53.

17. Ibid., p. 152.

18. Ibid.

19. Ibid., p. 153.

20. *Aufklärung für Kinder,* p. 193.

21. Michael Marrus and Robert Paxton, *Vichy et les Juifs* (Paris: Calmann-Lévy, 1981), p. 67.

22. Robert Paxton, *Vichy France: Old Guard and New Order, 1940–1944* (New York: Norton, 1972), p. 181.

23. Primo Levi, *Moments of Reprieve,* trans. Ruth Feldman (New York: Summit, 1979), p. 170. *King of the Jews* (New York: Avon, 1979) is the title of the remarkable novel Leslie Epstein has forged from the Rumkowski case.

24. Levi, *Moments of Reprieve,* p. 167.

25. Ibid.

26. Gershom Scholem, *Walter Benjamin,* p. 96.

27. Ibid., p. 97.

28. Ibid.; Gershom Scholem, *From Berlin to Jerusalem*, trans. Harry Zohn (New York: Schocken, 1980), p. 147. For a more positive recent assessment of Goldberg's influence, see Judith Friedlander, *Vilna on the Seine* (New Haven: Yale University Press, 1990), pp. 173–83.

29. Scholem, *Walter Benjamin*, p. 98. In January 1921 Benjamin wrote to Scholem that *Politik und Metaphysik*, by Erich Unger, a key member of the Goldberg circle, was "the most important writing on politics of this time." *Briefe* (Frankfurt: Suhrkamp, 1978), p. 252.

30. Scholem, *Walter Benjamin*, p. 98.

31. Primo Levi, *The Periodic Table*, trans. Raymond Rosenthal (New York: Schocken, 1984), pp. 79–95. For a consideration of Benjamin's work "under the sign of Saturn," see Susan Sontag, *Under the Sign of Saturn* (New York: Vintage, 1981), pp. 109–34.

32. Levi, *The Periodic Table*, p. 87.

33. See Gershom Scholem, "Walter Benjamin and His Angel," in *On Jews and Judaism in Crisis*, ed. W. Dannhauser (New York: Schocken, 1976), p. 209.

34. Levi, *The Periodic Table*, p. 88.

35. Ibid., p. 94.

36. Ibid., p. 95.

37. Ibid., p. 148.

38. Ibid., p. 156.

39. Ibid., p. 158.

40. Ibid.

41. See my "Trimethylamin: Notes on Freud's Specimen Dream," in *Untying the Text: A Post-Structuralist Reader*, ed. Robert Young (Boston: Routledge and Kegan Paul, 1981), pp. 177–88.

42. Levi, *The Periodic Table*, p. 214.

43. Ibid., p. 219.

44. Ibid., p. 223.

45. Levi, *Moments of Reprieve*, p. 172.

46. Levi, *The Periodic Table*, p. 35.

47. Ibid.

48. See Henry Hatfield, *Thomas Mann* (New York: New Directions, 1952), p. 77; Thomas Mann, *The Magic Mountain*, trans. H. T. Lowe-Porter (New York: Vintage, 1952), p. 461.

49. For a discussion of Thomas Mann's work in its relation to anti-Semitism, see Alfred Hoetzel, "Thomas Mann's Attitudes Toward Jews and Judaism: An Investigation of Biography and Oeuvre," in *Studies in Contemporary Jewry*, ed. Ezra Mendelsohn, vol. 6, (New York: Oxford University Press, 1990).

50. See Benjamin, "Conversations with Brecht," in *Reflections* (New York: Schocken, 1978), p. 208: "The day before yesterday we had a long and heated debate on my Kafka. Its basis: the charge that it advanced Jewish fascism." That opinion is analyzed by Robert Alter in *Necessary Angels: Tradition and Modernity in Kafka, Benjamin, and Scholem* (Cambridge: Harvard University Press, 1991).

51. Thomas Mann, *Dr. Faustus,* trans. H. T. Lowe-Porter (New York: Vintage, 1948), p. 284.

52. See Leslie Fiedler, *Fiedler on the Roof: Essays on Literature and Jewish Identity* (Boston: David Godine, 1991), p. 180.

INDEX

115